THE NATIONAL INSTITUTE OF
ECONOMIC AND SOCIAL RESEARCH

Occasional Papers
XXXIV

INTERNATIONAL INDUSTRIAL PRODUCTIVITY

A comparison of Britain, America and Germany

THE NATIONAL INSTITUTE OF ECONOMIC AND SOCIAL RESEARCH

2 DEAN TRENCH STREET, SMITH SQUARE, LONDON, SWIP 3HE

The National Institute of Economic and Social Research is an independent, non-profit-making body, founded in 1938. It has as its aim the promotion of realistic research, particularly in the field of economics. It conducts research by its own research staff and in cooperation with the universities and other academic bodies. The results of the work done under the Institute's auspices are published in several series, and a list of its recent publications will be found at the end of this volume.

INTERNATIONAL INDUSTRIAL PRODUCTIVITY

A comparison of Britain, America and Germany

A. D. SMITH
D. M. W. N. HITCHENS
and
S. W. DAVIES

CAMBRIDGE UNIVERSITY PRESS
CAMBRIDGE
LONDON NEW YORK NEW ROCHELLE
MELBOURNE SYDNEY

Published by the Press Syndicate of the University of Cambridge
The Pitt Building, Trumpington Street, Cambridge CB2 1RP
32 East 57th Street, New York, NY 10022, USA
296 Beaconsfield Parade, Middle Park, Melbourne 3206, Australia

First published 1982

Printed in Great Britain at
the Pitman Press, Bath

Library of Congress catalogue card number: 82–4348

British Library Cataloguing in Publication Data

Smith, A. D.
International industrial productivity.—
(Occasional papers/National Institute of
Economic and Social Research; 34)
1. Industrial productivity
I. Title II. Hitchens, D. M. W. N.
III. Davies, S. W. IV. Series
3338'.06 HD56

ISBN 0 521 24901 5

P.P.

CONTENTS

List of tables *page* ix
List of charts x
Preface xiii

PART I THE ANALYSIS OF SECTORAL PRODUCTIVITY DIFFERENTIALS

1 INTRODUCTION 3
Comparative industrial productivity 4
Sector and country coverage 6
Structure of the study 8

2 SECTORAL PRODUCTIVITY MEASUREMENT 10
The industry approach 10
Research developments 11
Labour productivity 12
Problems of measurement 14
Gross output productivity measures 15
Net output productivity measures 16
The measurement of labour inputs 17
Tracing changes in comparative productivity ratios 18
Aggregation of the sectoral results 18
Service sector estimates 19
Reliability of the results 19

3 COMPARATIVE INTERNATIONAL PRODUCTIVITY 20
Modifications to the results 20
Comparative productivity with alternative weighting systems 20
Hours of work and productivity ratios 22
The impact of double deflation 23
Structural and productivity effects 25
Their separation 25
Sectoral contributions to industrial productivity differences 27

Changes in productivity ratios 28
Recent developments 28
Long-term changes: an Anglo-American comparison 37

4 GENERAL INFLUENCES ON COMPARATIVE INDUSTRIAL PERFORMANCE 41
Absolute and comparative labour productivity 43
Comparative productivity and capital intensity 45
Comparative productivity and market size 48
Comparative productivity and labour force quality 49
Comparative productivity and strike action 51
Growth and productivity improvements 52

5 PRODUCTIVITY DIFFERENCES AND SECTORAL CHARACTERISTICS 56
Agriculture 56
Extractive industries 58
Manufacturing 61
Construction 66
Public utilities 67
Transport and communications 69

6 AN ANALYSIS OF MANUFACTURING PRODUCTIVITY RATIOS 75
Productivity ratios for individual manufacturing industries 75
Preliminary correlation analysis 80
The explanatory variables 82
Interpretation of the correlations 84
Regression analysis 86

7 CONCLUSIONS 90
The principal findings 90
Influences on productivity differentials 93
The findings and industrial policy 98

PART II THE MEASUREMENT OF PRODUCTIVITY DIFFERENTIALS

8 AGRICULTURE, FORESTRY AND FISHING 103
Structure and method 103
Measurement of agricultural output 104
The labour force 106
Comparative productivity in agriculture, forestry and fishing 107
Double deflated results 107
Contemporary productivity 109

9 EXTRACTIVE INDUSTRIES 110
Structure of the industry and method 110
Coal and 'other' mining and quarrying 111
Oil and gas extraction 113
Aggregation of sub-sector ratios 113
Comparative productivity in earlier years 114

10 MANUFACTURING INDUSTRY 115
Comparative US/UK productivity ratios, 1967–8 115
Comparative Germany/UK productivity ratios, 1967–8 117
Reliability of the results 121
Double deflated results 124
Contemporary productivity 125

11 THE CONSTRUCTION INDUSTRY 127
Structure of the industry 127
Measuring comparative productivity in construction 127
Comparative productivity 128
Double deflated results 130
Contemporary productivity 131
Reliability of the results 132

12 PUBLIC UTILITIES 134
Structure of the industry 134
Measuring comparative productivity 135
Gas 135
Electricity 137
Water 137
Other activities 138
Contemporary productivity 138

13 TRANSPORT AND COMMUNICATIONS 140
Structure of the industry 140
Measuring productivity in transport and communications 142
Sub-sectoral productivity comparisons 144
Railways 144
Local and road passenger transport 146
Road haulage 147
Sea transport, ports and inland waterways 148
Air transport 151
Posts and telecommunications 153
Aggregation of sub-sector ratios 156
Contemporary productivity 156

14 TECHNICAL NOTE 158
Gross output productivity comparisons 158
Net output productivity comparisons 160
Tracing changes in comparative productivity ratios 162
Aggregation of sectoral results 163

Index 167

TABLES

1.1 Comparative labour productivity, 1968–77 5
1.2 The sectoral structure of output and employment, 1976–7 7
3.1 Productivity ratios with alternative price weights 21
3.2 Productivity ratios adjusted for hours of work 23
3.3 Impact of double deflation on productivity ratios 24
3.4 National productivity ratios: a hypothetical example 25
3.5 Productivity and structural effects, 1977 26
3.6 Net sectoral contributions to international industrial productivity differences, 1977 28
3.7 Long-term changes in comparative productivity: US/UK 38
4.1 Sectoral labour productivity levels, 1977 43
4.2 Absolute and comparative labour productivity levels, 1977 44
4.3 Capital intensity and comparative productivity, 1973 46
4.4 Comparative capital intensity and productivity ratios 47
4.5 Relative market size, 1976–7 48
4.6 Comparative productivity and labour force quality, 1976 50
4.7 Comparative productivity and strike action, US/UK, 1974 51
4.8 Sectoral output and productivity changes, 1968–77 53
4.9 Sectoral productivity changes in relation to sectoral output changes 55
5.1 Agricultural yields and labour intensities, 1970 57
5.2 Comparative productivity in the extractive industries, 1968 and 1977 58
5.3 The structure of manufacturing industry 62
5.4 Comparative productivity in principal manufacturing industries, 1968 and 1976 63
5.5 Manufacturing industry output and productivity changes, US and UK, 1968–77 65
5.6 Manufacturing industry output and productivity changes, Germany and UK, 1968–76 66
5.7 Comparative productivity in public utilities 68
5.8 Labour productivity and the structure of transport 70
5.9 Comparative productivity in transport activities 72
6.1 Manufacturing industry comparative productivity ratios 1967–8 78
6.2 Manufacturing industry sample coverage 80
6.3 Associations between explanatory factors and productivity ratios 81
8.1 Structure of the agriculture, forestry and fishing sectors, 1974 103
8.2 Comparative productivity in agriculture, forestry and fishing, 1974 107
8.3 Double deflated comparative productivity in agriculture, forestry and fishing, 1974 108

8.4 Comparative productivity in agriculture, forestry and fishing, 1968–77 109
9.1 Employment structure of the extractive industries 110
9.2 Basic data for coal mining and 'other' mining 1967–8 111
9.3 Comparative productivity in coal mining and 'other' mining, 1967–8 112
9.4 Comparative productivity in oil and natural gas extraction, 1977 113
9.5 Comparative productivity in extractive industries, 1968–77 114
10.1 Comparative productivity in manufacturing industries, US/UK 1967–8 118
10.2 Comparative productivity in manufacturing industries, Germany/UK 1967–8 122
10.3 Comparative productivity in the manufacturing sector, 1968–77 126
11.1 Construction industry basic data, 1967–8 129
11.2 Comparative productivity in construction, 1967–8 130
11.3 Comparative productivity in construction, 1968–77 131
12.1 Public utilities basic data, 1975 134
12.2 Comparative productivity in public utilities, 1975 136
12.3 Comparative productivity in public utilities, 1968–77 139
13.1 Employment structure of transport and communications, 1970–2 140
13.2 Comparative railway productivity 145
13.3 Comparative productivity in local and road passenger transport 146
13.4 Comparative road haulage productivity 148
13.5 Comparative productivity in shipping 149
13.6 Comparative port productivity 150
13.7 Comparative airline productivity 152
13.8 Comparative airport productivity 152
13.9 Comparative productivity in postal services, US/UK, 1972 154
13.10 Comparative productivity in telecommunications, US/UK, 1972 155
13.11 Comparative productivity in posts and telecommunications, Germany/UK, 1970 155
13.12 Comparative productivity in transport and communications, 1968–77 157

SYMBOLS IN THE TABLES

... not available
— nil or negligible
n.a. not applicable

CHARTS

3.1 Comparative productivity ratios 1968–77: US/UK 29
3.2 Comparative productivity ratios 1968–77: Germany/UK 30
3.3 Output, employment and productivity changes, 1968–77: Agriculture 31
3.4 Output, employment and productivity changes, 1968–77: Extractive industries 32
3.5 Output, employment and productivity changes, 1968–77: Manufacturing 33
3.6 Output, employment and productivity changes, 1968–77: Construction 34
3.7 Output, employment and productivity changes, 1968–77: Utilities 35

3.8 Output, employment and productivity changes, 1968–77: Transport and Communications 36
6.1 The distribution of US/UK manufacturing industry productivity ratios, 1967–8 76
6.2 The distribution of Germany/UK manufacturing industry productivity ratios, 1967–8 77

Data in tables and charts with unspecified sources are taken from Part II.

PREFACE

As the National Institute of Economic and Social Research approaches its fiftieth anniversary it is appropriate that this latest of its studies should evoke a theme of one of its earliest: the pioneering work in international productivity studies, relating to the 1930s, produced by L. Rostas, *Comparative Productivity in British and American Industry.* The present study owes much in objective and methodology, but above all in inspiration, to this work.

Not that the theme of this early study, the measurement and analysis, sector by sector, of international differences in labour productivity, is in any sense 'dated'. British (and foreign) economists and politicians, now and for some decades, have been concerned and perhaps bemused by the comparatively poor productivity performance of the United Kingdom. The present study seeks to pinpoint the sectors of British industry where, in terms of labour productivity, our performance, compared with the United States and Germany, is especially bad, those where it is less unsatisfactory and, conceivably, those where it is good. The intention is that the findings should help to identify the factors which are responsible for Britain's unsatisfactory industrial performance and go some way towards guiding policy makers to an effective industrial strategy.

The present study is but one in a wider programme of productivity research which the National Institute has initiated. In particular it is hoped that research resources will enable the kind of international productivity comparisons made here for the industrial sector to be extended to service activities. The present research was financed in its entirety by the Leverhulme Trust, to which organisation the National Institute is very grateful.

The project was directed by Mr A. D. Smith, economic consultant at the National Institute. Mr D. M. W. N. Hitchens was involved on a full-time basis and Mr S. W. Davies, of the University of East Anglia, participated as a part-time consultant.

Mrs E. Campbell-Boross helped to compile the chapters concerned with productivity measurement in the extractive industries, manufacturing and public utilities mainly, though not exclusively, in the capacity of the team's German source consultant. Andrew White assisted in the task of 'matching' British and American manufacturing industries.

The Director of the Institute read and commented upon the study as it emerged. Mr S. J. Prais took a special interest in the project from inception to completion, providing constructive suggestions on all the aspects, measurement and analytical, of the work. Miss Deborah Paige – another pioneer of the approach adopted in the study – was kind enough to sacrifice some of her retirement time to provide invaluable advice on the more intricate productivity measurement problems. The Secretary of the Institute, Mrs K. Jones, and Mr G. F. Ray, also gave us the benefit of their comments. To all these individuals we are most grateful whilst, of course, absolving them from any shortcomings which the study might still retain.

We wish to express our sincere thanks also to the secretarial, computation and editorial staff of the National Institute. Inevitably a study such as this emerges from a considerable number of drafts and re-drafts which they have produced and re-produced with great fortitude and rare patience.

National Institute of Economic and Social Research A. D. SMITH

January 1982 D. M. W. N. HITCHENS

S. W. DAVIES

Part I

THE ANALYSIS OF SECTORAL PRODUCTIVITY DIFFERENTIALS

1

INTRODUCTION

It has been recognised for many years that, compared with the United States, Britain's industrial performance has been poor; in the last two decades it has also become true in relation to some other developed countries. The costs, social and economic, of this weakness have been much emphasised: a lack of international competitiveness and restricted living standards, together with detrimental implications for the pace of future economic growth. Not surprisingly therefore, many attempts have been made over the years to explain our predicament in terms of a wide variety of factors acting individually or in combination: ineffective management, labour force overmanning, poor industrial relations, insufficient research and development, inadequate investment, an impoverishment of national resources and ill-conceived government policies.

In this quest comparatively little attention has been devoted to the identification of those sectors which, in relation to performance in other countries, have reflected, respectively, the strengths and weaknesses of the British economy. Consequently, this study seeks to analyse our poor industrial performance by a route which has not been systematically attempted for many years.[1] In essence, the objective is to establish in which activities British performance has been comparatively bad and in which comparatively good, in order to determine whether the above strictures apply alike to all sectors of the British economy. For this purpose labour productivity has been measured for six activities – agriculture, extractive industries, manufacturing, construction, public utilities and transportation – and compared between the United Kingdom, United States and the Federal Republic of Germany in the years 1968 to 1977.

Such an inter-country, inter-sectoral comparison of productivity levels provides a basis for an explanation of the economy's performance which goes beyond the mere identification of comparatively weak and strong

[1] Earlier studies which sought, *inter alia*, to measure comparative industrial performance along similar lines were undertaken by L. Rostas, *Comparative Productivity in British and American Industry*, NIESR Occasional Paper XIII, Cambridge University Press 1948, and D. Paige and G. Bombach, *A Comparison of National Output and Productivity of the United Kingdom and the United States*, Paris, OEEC, 1959.

sectors. It enables the responsibility for differences in national productivity levels to be allocated between, on the one hand, variations in the structure of economic activity (between high and low labour productivity activities) and, on the other, inter-country contrasts in the productivity levels registered in a given sector. In turn, the latter sectoral comparative productivity ratios may be analysed and explained in terms of such variables as capital intensities, market sizes and rates of sectoral growth.

Within this study we are thus primarily concerned with measuring and explaining inter-country sectoral productivity differences. However, it should be recognised that the *implications* of these international sectoral productivity ratios extend beyond the identification of activities and factors principally responsible for good and bad national economic performance. The ratios which emerge are highly relevant for the economy's foreign trade performance and for the structure of the country's imports and exports. Levels and changes in sectoral unit labour costs, of which labour productivity is a basic ingredient, do much to determine both these patterns. Similarly, changes in sectoral productivity levels, taken in conjunction with developments in patterns of demand and output, effectively shape the economy's labour force, structure and composition.

COMPARATIVE INDUSTRIAL PRODUCTIVITY

Table 1.1 presents the principal results of this study. It shows the comparative labour productivity ratios (UK = 1·00) for the six non-service sectors, between the United Kingdom and the United States and between the United Kingdom and Germany, during the period 1968 to 1977. It also shows overall productivity ratios, which suggest that in 1977 American industrial productivity was 2·66 times better than Britain's, and Germany's 1·43 times better.

There is much similarity between the US/UK sectoral pattern of results and the Germany/UK pattern. It is clear that in 1977 British performance in the extractive industries and in public utilities was especially poor compared with both the American and German industries. Better performers, *vis-à-vis* both the United States and Germany, were British agriculture and transport, but only in the case of agriculture compared with Germany was our labour productivity absolutely higher. In both pairs of country comparisons relative productivities in British manufacturing of 2·91 and 1·52 were not far from the overall industrial ratios.

For analytical purposes it is unfortunate that the construction sector is the odd man out in these patterns – relative to the US it is our least

Table 1.1. *Comparative labour productivity, 1968–77*

UK = 1.00

	Agriculture	Extractive industries	Manu-facturing	Con-struction	Public utilities	Transport[a]	All industry
United States/United Kingdom							
1968	2·42	6·68	2·89	2·06	4·26	2·62	2·78
1969	2·47	6·65	2·89	1·86	4·15	2·54	2·75
1970	2·40	6·92	2·85	1·63	3·97	2·51	2·68
1971	2·30	6·84	2·94	1·59	3·83	2·49	2·72
1972	2·07	8·06	2·93	1·65	3·45	2·50	2·71
1973	2·11	6·64	2·80	1·65	3·19	2·43	2·59
1974	1·94	6·91	2·68	1·55	3·16	2·40	2·51
1975	2·22	5·94	2·82	1·65	3·21	2·52	2·66
1976	2·33	4·84	2·84	1·85	3·22	2·63	2·72
1977	2·09	3·42	2·91	1·70	3·07	2·64	2·66
Germany/United Kingdom							
1968	0·77	2·00	1·35	1·72	1·74	1·15	1·26
1969	0·72	2·08	1·40	1·70	1·82	1·18	1·29
1970	0·70	2·13	1·35	1·71	1·84	1·21	1·28
1971	0·69	2·12	1·33	1·63	1·83	1·17	1·26
1972	0·66	2·55	1·31	1·65	1·72	1·10	1·28
1973	0·75	2·25	1·34	1·70	1·73	1·02	1·29
1974	0·74	2·54	1·36	1·82	1·81	1·05	1·33
1975	0·79	2·32	1·40	1·93	1·89	1·06	1·36
1976	0·86	1·97	1·47	2·24	2·02	1·08	1·43
1977	0·82	1·51	1·52	2·18	1·89	1·14	1·43

[a] Unless designated otherwise, this sector embraces communications throughout the study.

unfavourable sector with a ratio of 1·70, relative to Germany our worst with a ratio of 2·18 – since it is the one for which productivity measurement is the most difficult and perhaps least reliable. Whether or not this somewhat paradoxical result is more than a statistical chimera is considered at a later stage.

It is not a principal objective of this study to direct attention to, or seek to explain, bilateral sectoral labour productivity ratios between the US and Germany: in all cases the methodology (for instance, choice of country price-weights) has sought to focus attention on British performance in relation to the other two economies. Nevertheless, United States/Germany productivity ratios are implied by the data in table 1.1. They suggest that in 1977, the overall US/Germany industrial ratio was 1·86. It would appear that America was especially good in agriculture (2·55), extractive industries (2·26) and transport and communications (2·32); and Germany comparatively good in public utilities (1·62) and absolutely better in construction (0·78) whilst the US/Germany manufacturing productivity ratio (1·91) differed little from the industrial average.

These sectoral patterns appear remarkably durable. In the case of the US/UK comparison the ranking of the sectoral ratios in 1977 was identical with that in 1968. And in the Germany/UK comparison the sectors which displayed above average productivity ratios in 1968, and those below average, were divided in the same way in 1977. However, thanks to an improvement in the British extractive industry and public utilities productivity *vis-à-vis* the United States, the spread of the US/UK sectoral productivity ratios has greatly diminished over recent years from one of 6·68 (extractive industries) ranging to 2·06 (construction) in 1968, to one of 3·42 (extractive industries) ranging to 1·70 (construction) in 1977.

A comparison with earlier studies suggests that, at least in the case of the US/UK comparison, the revealed sectoral pattern of labour productivity ratios has endured for several decades. As long ago as the 1930s our better performers were agriculture and construction, our worst the extractive industries and utilities. The same exercise reveals, again *vis-à-vis* the United States, that after a pronounced deterioration in the 1940s comparative British labour productivity has improved perceptibly, if gradually. Some confirmation of this trend is provided for the period 1968–77 by table 1.1. Over the same years, however, our industrial performance compared with Germany's has deteriorated significantly.

SECTOR AND COUNTRY COVERAGE

Most research in international productivity comparisons has focussed on the manufacturing sector to the neglect of other economic activities. This study seeks in some measure to redress this imbalance by measuring and analysing international labour productivity differences in certain non-manufacturing, as well as manufacturing, activities. Whilst the six major sectors covered are not all normally regarded as industrial, we shall for convenience refer throughout to the comparisons as those of 'industrial' productivity.

Although the data presented in table 1.2 are not entirely comparable between countries, they are sufficiently akin to demonstrate that these industrial sector comparisons embrace a high proportion of economic activity in all three economies, whether measured by output or employment. Highest coverage is recorded in Germany with 68 per cent of output and 59 per cent of employment found in the 'industrial' sector. In the United Kingdom the corresponding percentages are 63 and 49, and in the United States 52 and 40. Of the six individual sectors included in this study, manufacturing is comfortably the largest in all three countries, a factor which needs to be borne in mind when the reliability of the

Table 1.2. *The sectoral structure of output and employment, 1976–7*

	GDP in producers' values			Civilian employment		
	United Kingdom 1977 (£m)	United States 1977 ($th.m)	Federal Republic of Germany 1976 (DM m)	United Kingdom 1977 (th)	United States 1977 (th)	Federal Republic of Germany 1976 (th)
Agriculture	3447	52·0	32770	661	3383	1743
Extractive industries	3627	50.0	14690	350	848[a]	355
Manufacturing	35279	454·0	421580	7473	20603[a]	8784
Construction	8062	84·9	80640	1653	5504	1836
Public utilities	4296	47.1	32030	350	1041	215
Transport	10244	120.6	66480	1528	5089	1521
All industry	64955	808·6	648190	12015	36468	14454
All services[b]	37708	754·4	307260	12535	54078	10102
TOTAL	102663	1563·0	955450	24550	90546	24556
			Percentages			
Agriculture	3·4	3·3	3·4	2·7	3·7	7·1
Extractive industries	3·5	3·2	1·5	1·4	0·9	1·4
Manufacturing	34·4	29·0	44·1	30·4	22·8	35·8
Construction	7·9	5·5	8·4	6·7	6·1	7·5
Public utilities	4·2	3·0	3·4	1·4	1·1	0·9
Transport	10·0	7·7	7·0	6·2	5·6	6·2
All industry	63·3	51·7	67·8	48·9	40·3	58·9
All services	36·7	48·3	32·2	51·1	59·7	41·1
TOTAL	100·0	100·0	100·0	100·0	100·0	100·0

Sources: United Nations, *Yearbook of National Accounts Statistics 1978* and OECD, *Labour Force Statistics, 1966–77*.

[a] Estimated from a combined total for mining, quarrying and manufacturing.

[b] Including deduction for imputed bank service charges.

overall results is considered since labour productivity measurement is comparatively straightforward in this activity.

Indeed, whilst the structural compositions of the three industrial economies presented in table 1.2 are far from identical, they are basically very similar, a conclusion which should perhaps hardly occasion much surprise in the context of a comparison of three developed countries. This similarity is significant when an attempt is made to distinguish between the 'structural' and 'productivity' contributions to the overall performance of the three economies.

With such sectoral coverage the study goes much of the way towards ascertaining which activities display relatively good or bad labour productivity performances at the national level. However the exclusion of services – distribution, finance, public administration, professional and miscellaneous services – means that a complete and definitive answer to this question cannot at this juncture be provided. On the basis of the data in table 1.2 such activities account in the United Kingdom for some 37 per cent of output and 51 per cent of employment. In the United States the corresponding percentages are 48 and 60 and in Germany 32 and 41.

The National Institute is now implementing a work programme which will extend international productivity comparisons to the service sectors. In the meantime very approximate estimates, which in the circumstances are inevitably crude in nature, have been made for US/UK and Germany/UK differentials in service activities to complete, *pro tem*, for the economy as a whole, the picture portrayed in table 1.1. They suggest that for the whole economy labour productivity differentials would be somewhat less than the industrial productivity ratios shown in table 1.1. In the case of the US/UK comparison the 1977 differential would appear to be of the order of 2·0 and, in the case of the Germany/UK ratio, a little under 1·4.

The United States was chosen as one of the comparison countries on the grounds that it was for many years the pace setter for technological and productivity improvements and traditionally has come to play the role of bench-mark in such international comparisons. The German economy was selected for somewhat different reasons. Not only does it represent one of our principal competitors and standards of comparison within the European Economic Community but also, unlike the United States, its economic performance has continued to improve significantly *vis-à-vis* our own from a position that until comparatively recently was not too dissimilar.

STRUCTURE OF THE STUDY

Part II of this study comprises six chapters outlining the measurement of labour productivity and comparative productivity in each of the selected sectors: agriculture, extractive industries, manufacturing, construction, public utilities and transport.[1] Part I, chapters 1 to 7, is concerned with the presentation and analysis of the results.

In chapter 2, the basic concepts and methods of measurement used to quantify labour productivity and comparative productivity are outlined and a Technical Note at the end of this study describes these methods in more detail. Chapter 3 considers the comparative sectoral productivity ratios which emerge between the UK and the US, the UK and Germany, for the years 1968 to 1977. Certain aspects of the results are explored: the extent to which the results are modified by variations in

[1] More detailed descriptions of measurement methods for each sector are available, on request, from the National Institute.

methodology, the degree to which industrial productivity differences are attributable to contrasts in the economies' structures rather than to productivity effects *per se*, together with long term and more recent trends in sectoral productivities and productivity ratios.

Chapter 4 enquires whether the international productivity differentials which emerge for the six non-service sectors are associated with the kind of economic factor to which attention is automatically directed in this context, such as inter-country differences in capital intensities, market sizes, labour force quality and growth rates. In chapter 5 the results are subject to sector by sector scrutiny to determine the role of special industry characteristics, including the sub-sectoral make-up of the activity, in shaping the measured productivity differentials. Attention is focussed on the manufacturing sector in chapter 6. The analysis in this latter chapter is facilitated by the fact that productivity levels and ratios have been measured for 117 component manufacturing industries in the case of the UK/US comparison and for 69 in the UK/Germany comparison. The principal conclusions of the study are assembled in chapter 7.

2

SECTORAL PRODUCTIVITY MEASUREMENT

THE INDUSTRY APPROACH

To understand the need for the present study something should be said about the way economists measure differences between countries in national economic well-being and performance. In recent years most studies have approached this problem from the point of view of a country's final expenditure – 'the expenditure approach'. With this approach, all goods and services bought for consumption and investment purposes in two countries are valued at common prices and the two resulting totals divided by the respective population sizes to yield measures of real income per head in the two countries. For this purpose it is necessary only to consider those goods or services which enter final expenditure: bread that is eaten by consumers, machines in which producers invest. Items that are produced for intermediate purposes (for example the steel that is destined to be an input into the final production of cars) can be ignored since we are concerned with the net output of the economy as a whole. In practical terms this 'expenditure approach' is easier to implement than the one adopted in this study – the 'industry approach'.

However the limitations of the 'expenditure approach' are exposed when we seek to discover which sector of the economy contributes most to a national superiority or shortfall in productivity compared with another country. Also, final consumption by a community is not confined to the country's own production, but includes expenditure on imports. When assessing sectoral performance, that part of production which is exported needs to be taken into account. If we wish to track down the sectoral sources of a failing in productivity, it is clearly necessary to calculate productivity individually for each industry – from its net output and labour force – prior to comparison with the performance of its counterpart in other countries.

It should be appreciated that a measure of comparative international performance at the overall economy level derived from this 'industry approach' will not be identical with the measure of comparative economic well-being yielded by the 'expenditure approach'. In the first place imports and exports are treated differently as explained above.

Secondly, the denominator in the 'industry approach' is a labour force figure, in the 'expenditure approach' a measure of population size.

RESEARCH DEVELOPMENTS

There have been few studies based on the 'industry approach'.[1] Two works, especially, stand out: the comparisons made first by Rostas, and secondly by Paige and Bombach, of sectoral productivity levels in the British and American economies.[2] At the time of these studies, labour productivity comparisons were directed at two basic objectives, the provision of sectoral components for an assessment of relative national productivity and welfare levels and the identification of individual sectors responsible for comparatively low, or high, national living standards.

To be precise, Rostas sought to 'compare . . . output per head in several branches of the national economy in order to build up a picture of how output per head compares in the national economy as a whole of the different countries'. He also used the international productivity relatives obtained for some thirty-odd industries as a basis for explaining British and American productivity differentials.[3] Similarly, Paige and Bombach attempted to assess and compare per capita national income levels by the 'industry method': 'our object has been to present a comparison of the total real product in the two countries'. But like Rostas, Paige and Bombach appreciated that the significance of the 'industry method' lies as much in the manner in which it permits sectoral sources of national productivity differences to be identified, as in the resulting comparisons of per capita national income.[4]

Since these two works, the measurement and analysis of international sectoral productivity differentials has been largely neglected.[5] A major reason for this neglect is to be found in a technique which was developed (during the 1950s) by Gilbert and Kravis, which has proved more effective than the industry approach for achieving one of the two objectives specified above: assessing, and comparing, per capita real national product. The method – the 'expenditure approach' referred to

[1] A wide ranging survey of research developments and methods in this and related fields has been undertaken by I. B. Kravis, 'A survey of international comparisons of productivity', *The Economic Journal*, Vol. 86, No. 341, March 1976.

[2] L. Rostas, *Comparative Productivity*; and D. Paige and G. Bombach, *A Comparison of National Output*.

[3] Rostas, *op. cit.*, pp. 1 and 2.

[4] 'Of far greater importance . . . is the new information made available by the study on the relative position of individual sectors', Paige and Bombach, *op. cit.*, pp. 17 and 57.

[5] Two exceptions are noted below: the interest which has been lavished on the manufacturing sector and its component industries; and occasional international comparisons embracing certain non-manufacturing activities.

above – consists in deflating to a common currency valuation the finely divided elements of final expenditure by appropriate international purchasing power parities.[1] This line of research has culminated in two reports which have emerged from the United Nations International Comparison Project.[2] As a result comprehensive *per capita* expenditure and national income data are now available for many countries, developed and developing, over a number of years.

The measurement and analysis of international sectoral productivity differences has followed quite a separate line of development, the principal characteristic of which is an almost exclusive concern with the manufacturing sector. Typically, work of this *genre* entails the selection of a number of manufacturing industries for which reasonably reliable international productivity comparisons can be made.[3] The industries so selected frequently constitute a comparatively small proportion of the manufacturing sector, let alone of national economic activity. Only occasionally have attempts been made in recent years – by Mensink for instance[4] – to undertake international productivity comparisons for sectors other than manufacturing. Part of the explanation for this neglect lies in the more difficult conceptual and practical problems posed in the context of international comparisons when productivity measurement is extended beyond manufacturing activities.

LABOUR PRODUCTIVITY

The end product of the measurement sections of this study are sectoral

[1] M. Gilbert and I. B. Kravis, *An International Comparison of National Products and the Purchasing Power of Currencies*, Paris, OEEC, 1954; and Milton Gilbert and Associates, *Comparative National Products and Price Levels: A Study of Western Europe and the United States*, Paris, OEEC, 1958.

[2] Irving B. Kravis, Zoltan Kenessy, Alan Heston and Robert Summers, *A System of International Comparisons of Gross Product and Purchasing Power*, John Hopkins University Press, Baltimore and London, 1975; and Irving B. Kravis, Alan Heston and Robert Summers, *International Comparisons of Real Product and Purchasing Power*, International Bank for Reconstruction and Development, United Nations International Comparison Project: Phase II, Baltimore, John Hopkins University Press, 1978.

[3] See, for instance, M. Frankel, *British and American Manufacturing Productivity; A Comparison and Interpretation*, Bureau of Economic and Business Research, University of Illinois Bulletin 81, University of Illinois Press, 1957; G. J. A. Mensink, *Comparisons of Labour Productivity in the United Kingdom and the Netherlands, 1958*, Netherlands Central Bureau of Statistics, Statistical Studies No. 18, 1966; E. C. West, *Canada-United States Price and Productivity Differences in Manufacturing Industries, 1963*, Staff Study No. 32 prepared for the Economic Council of Canada, Ottawa, Queen's Printer 1971; K. Yukizawa, *Japanese and American Manufacturing Productivity: An International Comparison of Physical Output per Head*, Discussion Paper No. 087, Kyoto Institute of Economic Research, Kyoto University, March 1975; R. E. Caves, 'Productivity differences among industries', in R. E. Caves and Lawrence B. Krause (Eds), *Britain's Economic Performance*, Brookings Institution, Washington DC, 1980; and S. J. Prais, *Productivity and Industrial Structure; A Study of Manufacturing Industry in Britain, Germany and the United States*, Cambridge University Press, 1982.

[4] *Op. cit.*

labour productivity levels and international comparisons thereof. Virtually all these results are couched in terms of output per man year; only in chapter 3 are they modified for differences in hours of work.

Over the years so many studies of this kind have been concerned with labour productivity measurement that the advantages and limitations of this concept need hardly be spelt out in detail. The conventional measurement and analysis of labour productivity is grounded in, and justified by, two fundamental bases. At the national level, output per man, and by extension, output per head of the population, is the basic determinant of living standards. At the sectoral level, since labour costs bulk large in many economic activities, differences in labour productivity levels are a major determinant of inter-industry costs and international competitiveness.

On the other hand, whilst international differences in labour productivity may exert a strong influence on international contrasts in economic efficiency they are by no means identical concepts. Strictly any measure of economic efficiency would need to take account of the mixture of resources and factors available to the country and the manner and proportions in which they are combined to produce the blend of outputs signalled by the community. Nor should labour productivity measures be confused with total productivity in which factors of production other than labour are accommodated in the denominator of the productivity measure. Only in the case of raw materials has an attempt been made – and then a fairly crude one[1] – to allow for the usage of factors other than labour. As it is, the contributions to output of other factors of production – capital especially – do much to *explain* the international sectoral productivity differentials which emerge. The number and nature of the machines with which a manufacturing operative works, the quality of the roads on which a truck driver operates, will clearly influence the scale of their outputs and the levels of their productivity.

Indeed it should be emphasised that in a productivity analysis such as this there is no intention to compare like situations with like, nor would much be learned from such an approach in the present context. If all factors and circumstances are identical in a given productivity comparison then, by definition, the comparison would yield a ratio of unity. In the case of inter-plant comparisons, standardising for all but one or two factors may serve the useful purpose of identifying their individual contributions to output.

But that is not at all the intention of the present exercise. We are seeking to measure differences in national – or at least 'industrial' –

[1] Because of unsatisfactory results obtained with the 'double deflation' technique.

labour productivity, and to explain the results on the bases of individual sectoral performances. This implies that whilst it is necessary to make allowance on the output side for differences in product mix,[1] the contrasts in the results which emerge should reflect the full gamut of factors which influence and explain differences in national productivity levels. This means that the impact on the US/UK productivity ratio of environmental factors which enable a larger proportion of coal, in the US compared with the UK, to be mined from (higher productivity) opencast workings rather than (lower productivity) mines must be given full rein. Factors such as these do much to shape differences in international productivity levels and living standards.

It must be emphasised that there is no implication in this study that labour productivity should be maximised in all sectors at all costs. As explained above other factors of production play an important role in determining output and labour productivity levels, and it may be possible to raise the latter only by disproportionately large increases in other inputs. Moreoever, as is demonstrated in chapter 3, the manner in which inter-country labour productivity ratios at the national level are derived from, and determined by, international sectoral productivity ratios is by no means as straightforward as might seem at first blush. It is possible for one country's comparative sectoral labour productivity ratios to be inferior to another's, alongside a national labour productivity performance which is better. Notwithstanding such qualifications, it is clear that sectoral labour productivity performances and the factors, economic and technological, which shape them, are the principal determinants of a country's comparative standard of living.

PROBLEMS OF MEASUREMENT

In this section we consider the problems that are posed by the measurement, and international comparison, of sectoral labour productivity levels, and describe the measurement methods that have been used.[2] Attention is focussed on the general, common, elements of the

[1] Which, in cases such as transport services with their associated differences in 'terminal' and 'distance' elements, can be quite complex.

[2] Although the measurement of international comparative productivity levels is a field of economic research less developed than many others, over the years there has been an accumulation of considerable experience in measurement methodology. These methods have recently been the subject of an admirable survey by Kravis ('A survey of international comparisons of productivity'), perhaps the most striking feature of which is the variety of methodologies that have been attempted at various times by different people. The methods vary, *inter alia*, in their bases (physical and value) in the levels to which they pertain (national, sectoral, industry, firm, plant) and in whether or not they are concerned with single, or multiple, factor inputs. The basic methodology used in this study is well established, though it required further development in certain areas to deal with specific measurement problems which arose.

methods employed. Contrasts between the conditions and concepts appropriate for the various sectors examined, and between the nature and reliability of the various data sources used, inevitably dictate that all elements of a basic methodology cannot be applied in their entirety to each activity in each of the three countries. Whilst principal exceptions to the common approach are noted below, detailed variations are described in the relevant chapters of Part II. Also questions considered in this section are explored in greater detail in the Technical Note.

Gross output productivity measures

In a few activities it is possible to relate the output of a single, reasonably homogeneous, product to an identifiable labour force. In coal mining, for instance, it is a fairly straightforward procedure to measure tons of coal produced per man and to compare the results between countries.[1] Typically, however, the output of any productive unit – plant, firm, industry – consists of a series of, often very similar, products, the output of which can be related to a labour force figure only *in toto*, not individually. In the case of the motor vehicle industry it is impossible from census of production data to identify those workers who are exclusively responsible, respectively, for the production of Rolls-Royce cars and Metros, although the labour force associated with the combined output of cars can be measured. Similarly, only the total combined output of wheat, pork, eggs, potatoes, apples etc., can be related to a single agricultural labour force input and on the railways it is impossible to separate the workers responsible for the transportation of passengers from those handling goods.

Since the proportions in which the various output components are produced in any given activity differ between countries, it is necessary to aggregate the various items before international comparisons of output per man can be made. The obvious, and conventionally accepted, method is to use a series of weights based on the relative prices of the items in question, weights which broadly reflect the relative amounts of economic resources embodied in the various products and their utilities to the community. Because relative prices differ between countries, the outcome of such an output – and productivity – comparison will vary, depending on whether the prices used are those of the 'home' or 'other' country, though normally this discrepancy will not be very large. Where feasible, calculations have been made on both sets of weights and the results compared in chapter 3.

[1] Labour productivity measures based essentially on physical units have also been adopted for instance in the case of oil and gas extraction, water supply, road haulage, ports, shipping activities, airlines and airports.

Identical results for such an output and productivity comparison can be obtained by an alternative sequence of calculations. If the value of the 'other' country's output, expressed in the 'other' country's currency, is standardised, for comparison purposes, in the 'home' country's currency by means of an appropriately constructed international price ratio, the outcome is equivalent to weighting each country's physical units of output with the chosen price weights.[1] Since this 'deflation' approach has certain technical advantages, it has been adopted in this study for most comparisons.

Net output productivity measures

Measures of total and *per capita* national product derived by the 'expenditure approach' avoid double counting of intermediate goods by focussing on final expenditure categories. The corresponding requirement in the 'industry approach' is that real *net* output, and real *net* output per man, must be measured, if the totals aggregated over sectors are not to involve double counting and are to sum to a meaningful overall measure of comparative productivity for the industrial economy. In turn this implies that some allowance be made for the sector's consumption of inputs from other sectors.

The elimination from gross output of the usage of intermediate raw materials has implications for the interpretation of international labour productivity differentials. For real net output per man depends, *inter alia*, on the quantity and quality of the raw materials being processed. It is easy to conceive, for instance, that the nature of a car industry may differ significantly between two countries in such a way that in one the car is wholly made from the iron ore to the final product, whilst in the second country the industry is concerned mainly with assembling components bought in from other sectors. If the same number of cars were made by the same number of people in both countries, then a gross output, cars per head, productivity comparison would show the two countries on par, but would be highly misleading and quite unfair to the former country. Thus, by comparing productivity on the basis of *net* output per head, one of the factors which determine comparative productivity levels is, in principle, eliminated.

One method of allowing for raw material usage is the 'double deflation' technique. By this method real gross outputs are standardised for comparison in a common currency by the method described in the previous section, and from these are deducted real raw material usages obtained by an analogous procedure: values of raw material usage being deflated, for the given industry in the two countries, to a common

[1] See Technical Note.

standardised basis by means of an appropriate international raw material price index.

In view of the manner in which this method tends to magnify errors in the basic data,[1] it has not been used extensively in this study. However, on occasion, specific, *ad hoc*, measures of labour productivity and comparative labour productivity, have been made on the basis of double deflated net outputs. They have been attempted where it is thought that allowing for variations between countries in the 'real' level of inputs could significantly affect the results, and where input data (both quantities and prices) are such that the procedure is feasible. Such double deflated results have been calculated, for instance, for agriculture. Primary attention, however, has been focussed on the net output labour productivity comparisons described below. Where they have been derived, double deflated measures are compared with the basic productivity ratios largely as a test of the sensitivity of the results.

The method adopted for most comparisons consists of deflating to a standardised basis the net output values of an industry in the two countries, using the gross output price indices referred to in the previous section. Inherent in this approach is the assumption that, for the activity in question, the relationship between the average cost of raw materials in the same two countries is identical with the gross output price index. The method is further considered in the Technical Note.

The measurement of labour inputs

The measurement of labour inputs normally presents fewer conceptual and practical problems than output measurement. Moreover, undue refinement of labour inputs has not been attempted in this study, attention being restricted, for the most part, to comparisons of net output per man year. Nor have any adjustments been made for inter-sectoral or international differences in the 'quality' of labour inputs as reflected in skill variations or the composition of the labour force. Consequently differences in all such labour force characteristics help to determine the comparative labour productivity ratios which emerge.

The procedures adopted for measuring labour inputs are not uniform – nor uniformly manageable – for each of the sectors covered. The exercise proves to be relatively straightforward, for instance, in the case of manufacturing. In contrast labour force measurement in agriculture is actually more difficult than output measurement, because of the importance of part-time and self employment.

[1] See the Technical Note.

Tracing changes in comparative productivity ratios

Resource and data limitations render it impracticable to measure directly labour productivity by industry, sub-sector and sector, in each of the three countries, for each year. However, there is much interest in analysing changes in, as well as levels of, comparative productivity ratios. This analytical requirement is bolstered by essentially practical considerations. Not surprisingly, it was found that the availability, detail and quality, of relevant statistics varied greatly from year to year, with a pattern that is not common for the six sectors and three countries. Thus, to achieve maximum reliability, and in some cases to permit any productivity measurement whatsoever, it was necessary to choose different base years for the principal productivity calculations in the various sectors.

These various base year labour productivity measures are brought forward to 1977, or taken back to 1968 as the case dictated, by real output and labour force indices relating to the country and sector in question. The indices used and their application are described in Part II and the Technical Note.

Aggregation of the sectoral results

Aggregation of industry and sub-sectoral results into a labour productivity measure for each sector, and of the latter into a measure for the complete non-service economy poses problems, conceptual and practical, of rather unexpected subtlety. The appropriate procedure is to calculate *first*, for each country, the overall absolute productivity level, (standardised) net output per man. This is a weighted average of component sectoral (standardised) productivity levels, with each activity's share of the labour force as weights. At a second stage, the international aggregate productivity ratio is obtained by relating these overall national productivity levels to each other.

Certain features and properties of this aggregation procedure should be mentioned. First, the aggregate international productivity ratios which emerge are influenced not only by the ratios of the component sectors but also by differences in the industrial structures of the three countries. Secondly, the aggregate ratio is not simply a weighted average of the sectoral ratios. Thirdly, it is conceivable, as shown in chapter 3, for the aggregate ratio to lie outside the range of the sectoral ratios.

Fourthly, it is a prerequisite of the aggregation procedure that for each sector, in each country, there is available a (standardised) value of net output per head. Because of certain data deficiencies such values were not always automatically available in those cases where the productivity comparisons were based directly on physical units of output. To deal with this problem, the 'reverse valuation technique' was developed. This technique is described in the Technical Note, where the aggregation procedure is considered in rather more detail.

SERVICE SECTOR ESTIMATES

To complete the picture, the industrial productivity ratios were adjusted by estimates of comparative international productivity in the service sector, yielding the overall economy level ratios for the US/UK and Germany/UK presented in chapter 1. These estimates, necessarily crude in nature, were derived from three alternative calculations of the service sector ratio: two of them based on a deflation of service sector net outputs using Kravis price indices, the third adopting the arbitrary assumption that service sector ratios lie midway between unity and the observed industrial ratios. The results suggest that in 1970 the US/UK service sector ratio might have fallen between 1·43 and 1·83; and the Germany/UK ratio between 1·14 and 1·22. In terms of the overall economy level labour productivity for 1977, these results point towards US/UK and Germany/UK ratios of 2·0 and rather less than 1·4 respectively.

RELIABILITY OF THE RESULTS

It would be wrong to claim an unduly high reliability for the labour productivity measures and comparisons presented in this study. In order to measure and compare productivity for all the activities covered the degree of detail and precision with which the work could be pursued was inevitably restricted. In view of the breadth of the study, major reliance was perforce placed on secondary sources, and primary data pertaining to individual activities could only occasionally be tapped. Additionally, the requirements placed upon the estimation of productivity levels within the context of international comparability may mean that the result obtained for a given activity in a given country will not necessarily coincide with the industry's self assessment. In terms of the country comparisons, it is felt that errors in the results obtained for the Germany/UK comparison may be somewhat greater, especially in relation to the productivity differentials which emerge, than in the case of the US/UK comparison.

Even so, experimentation with the data presented in subsequent chapters suggests that the results are fairly robust: even relatively substantial modifications to the productivity estimates for component activities seem to have comparatively little effect on the sectoral results.

3

COMPARATIVE INTERNATIONAL PRODUCTIVITY

MODIFICATIONS TO THE RESULTS

The principal results which emerge from this study have been summarised in table 1.1 and briefly considered in chapter 1, whilst factors bearing on the statistical reliability of the results are identified in the relevant chapters of Part II. Although, as explained in the preceding chapter, complete reliability is not claimed for the sectoral labour productivity ratios which emerge, it is not thought that the margins of error involved are such that they would cloud the basic inter-sectoral, inter-country, picture which table 1.1 reveals. There are however certain conceptual qualifications that might systematically affect the received picture which merit further consideration. In particular the overall industrial ratios might be significantly modified when account is taken of the use of 'other country' price weights rather than British, differences between the United Kingdom, United States and Germany in hours of work and productivity measures based on the double deflation technique.

Comparative productivity with alternative weighting systems

It is frequently necessary when comparing labour productivity between two countries to add together outputs of different products. In such circumstances the normal practice, and the one mainly adopted in the present study, is to aggregate the various items using relative prices as weights. Because relative prices usually differ between countries, the method yields two sets of output and productivity results, one on 'own country price weights', the second on 'other country price weights'. Neither method can be viewed in any absolute sense as the correct one, discrepancies between them reflecting essentially the 'index number problem'. However, the principal results of this study, including those set out in table 1.1, are those derived using 'own country' British price weights.

Nevertheless for those sectors and sub-sectors where it proved possible, productivity levels were measured on both concepts. These alternative measures are assembled in table 3.1 to help ascertain the sensitivity of the sectoral pattern of ratios shown in table 1.1, whether or not the

Table 3.1. *Productivity ratios with alternative price weights*

UK = 1·00

	Year	UK Prices	'Other' country prices	Ratio of results
US/UK				
Agriculture	1974	1·94	1·79	1·08
Extractive (excluding oil and gas)	1967–8	5·45	5·09	1·07
Manufacturing	1967–8	2·76	2·52	1·10
Construction	1967–8	2·00	1·88	1·06
Germany/UK				
Agriculture	1974	0·74	0·74	1·00
Extractive (excluding oil and gas)	1967–8	1·82	1·64	1·11
Manufacturing	1967–8	1·23	1·15	1·07
Construction	1967–8	1·74	1·53	1·14

Source: See part II.

results are changed in a common direction when 'other country price weights' are used, and the extent to which the overall industrial productivity comparisons are modified.

The table reveals that in all eight cases British productivity is as good, or better, on 'other country price weights' than on British weights, reflecting the well-established phenomenon that domestic prices tend to be relatively low for those products where output is relatively large and vice versa. Secondly, although the effect works systematically in one direction, it is not unduly large: the results suggest that, based on these activities, it would not exceed 10 per cent overall. Thirdly, the use of alternative weights appears to have little impact on the sectoral pattern of international productivity ratios.[1]

These conclusions are basically confirmed by an inspection of the results obtained for individual manufacturing industries. Productivity ratios were obtained on both sets of country weights in 97 of the component manufacturing industries in the US/UK comparison. In no more than 16 of these was the differential unexpected in the sense that

[1] It is instructive to compare the above alternative US/UK productivity ratios with those measured by Paige and Bombach, (*A Comparison of National Output*, p. 21) for 1950.

	UK prices	US prices	Ratio of results
Agriculture	2·22	1·93	1·15
Fuels	7·69	6·12	1·26
Manufacturing	2·92	2·56	1·14
Transport	4·12	2·53	1·63

The excessive transport differential is probably explained by the effect of the very different relative prices of freight and passenger traffic on the two railway systems.

British productivity was even lower using US price weights, and the correlation coefficient between the two sets of results was as high as +0·89. In the Germany/UK manufacturing comparison measures using the alternative price weights were derived for 54 component industries and only 11 of these were perverse, the correlation coefficient being +0·86.[1]

It is also relevant in the present context that the aggregation procedure used for deriving overall industrial productivity ratios is based on British sectoral contributions to GDP – effectively that is, with British net output price weights. The impact of using 'other country price weights' has therefore been tested using US sectoral contributions to GDP. For 1976 there emerges an overall industrial ratio of 2·65 compared with 2·72 when British weights are used. The impact is thus again small and in the anticipated direction: we emerge better using 'other country' rather than our 'own country' price weights.

Hours of work and productivity ratios

Our primary concern is with comparative productivity based on output per man year. Again, it is pertinent to enquire, if only in a rather general way, what would be the effect on the overall results and on the sectoral pattern of international productivity ratios if some allowance were made for the fact that hours of work may differ between the United Kingdom, United States and Germany.

Although the modification in table 3.2 is based on differences in weekly hours, it may be accepted as a rough adjustment for total annual hours worked since the data suggest that holiday provisions in the UK are generally less generous than those in the other two countries.

The table indicates that British industrial productivity performance is even poorer compared with either the United States or Germany, when measured by output per man hour rather than per man. However the adjustment would not appear to be unduly large, yielding industrial productivity ratios about 10 per cent worse in the case of the US/UK comparison and substantially less than that in the Germany/UK comparison,[2] whether based on 1968 or 1977. Lack of comparable coverage in the available international statistics precludes much of an adjustment to individual sectors. It is interesting, however, that table 3.2

[1] In the case of both the US/UK and Germany/UK comparisons, food industries figure prominently among the perverse results. This may well reflect the distortion which in these activities taxes and subsidies exert on the relevant product prices. Whilst alternative weighting systems disturb the overall pattern of results only to a minor extent, they may have a disproportionately large impact in individual cases.

[2] At the time of Rostas' study, the late 1930s, the impact of this adjustment on the US/UK comparison was in the same direction but much larger – raising the manufacturing ratio by as much as 27 per cent (*Comparative Productivity*, p. 29).

Table 3.2. *Productivity ratios adjusted for hours of work*

UK = 1·00

	1968		1977	
	Unadjusted ratio	Hours adjusted ratio	Unadjusted ratio	Hours adjusted ratio
US/UK				
Manufacturing	2·89	3·09	2·91	3·00
Construction	2·06	2·62	1·70	2·06
All industry[a]	2·78	3·09	2·66	2·98
Germany/UK				
Manufacturing	1·35	1·36	1·52	1·52
Construction	1·72	1·86	2·18	2·37
All industry[a]	1·26	1·30	1·43	1·47

Sources: Table 1.1 and ILO *Yearbook of Labour Statistics*

[a] Based on a weighted average of hours worked in certain extractive industries, manufacturing and construction.

points to a much better American performance in construction when hours of work are taken into account – though even with such an allowance the sector would still rank lowest in relation to both the British and German economies.

The impact of double deflation

Double deflation is a technical aspect of a phenomenon that excites considerable interest in the context of international competitiveness, especially between Europe and the United States; the allegation is that because of America's greater degree of self-sufficiency in raw materials etc, and because of Federal government action to hold down the price of oil and gas – and thus fuel costs and inputs in the chemical and textile industries – industrial activities in the US have enjoyed a head start in competitiveness. The corollary of this in the present context is that low relative prices for US inputs may encourage a comparatively large usage of them per unit of output, in effect substituting for manpower and boosting labour productivity. In principle, allowance would be made for this in our measure by double deflation: by deflating to a £ sterling figure with appropriate international price indices both gross output and costs of raw materials to yield, as a balance, standardised net output.

For reasons explained in chapter 2 and the Technical Note, and especially because of the intrinsic unreliability of the methodology currently available for this procedure, the double deflation technique has not been systematically applied in this study. However double deflation was attempted in certain sectors in particular years – mainly

Table 3.3. *Impact of double deflation on productivity ratios*

UK = 1·00

Sector	Year	Prices	Unadjusted ratio	Double deflated ratio
US/UK				
Agriculture	1974	UK prices	1·94	2·10
		US prices	1·79	1·90
Manufacturing (total)	1967–8	US prices	2·52	2·95
Manufacturing (selected industries)[a]	1967–8	UK prices	2·63	1·99
		US prices	2·53	1·83
Construction	1967–8	US prices	1·88	1·70
Germany/UK				
Agriculture	1974	UK prices	0·74	0·73
		German prices	0·74	0·71

Source: Chapters 8, 10 and 11.
[a] Based on 14 selected industries.

for the US/UK comparisons – where it was thought it might introduce a significant modification (as in agriculture) and where some of the requisite data were available. The results are assembled in table 3.3

These results are motley to say the least. Both the adjustment for different price weights and hours were systematic in that the effect appeared to be of a similar order of magnitude and in the same direction in all sectors, leaving the basic pattern more or less undisturbed. An adjustment for weights would, overall, improve Britain's comparative performance by about a tenth, that for hours would tend to reduce it by no more than the same amount. Nothing like such systematic impacts can be traced in table 3.3. If the results are taken at their face value in relation to the United States, then British agriculture emerges rather worse with double deflation (though the original ratios are not greatly disturbed), construction rather better (though again not by much). But the shortcomings of the adjustment are made plain by the results for manufacturing which would suggest that the British performance would appear much better with one double deflation technique, much worse with another.[1] The essential indeterminancy of the adjustment reflects the tendency of double deflation to magnify statistical errors in the residual net output which emerges.

[1] A similar lack of pattern was evident in the findings of Paige and Bombach, *A Comparison of National Output*, who pursued the adjustment more assiduously than the present authors. Whilst the Paige-Bombach comparisons are not wholly on par with those given in table 3.3 they suggest that British agricultural productivity shows up worse with double deflation, extractive industries and the utilities rather better, and the impact on transport depends on the prices used.

STRUCTURAL AND PRODUCTIVITY EFFECTS

Their separation

The overall comparative productivity ratios measured in table 1.1 are in part determined by the individual ratios for the six component sectors, the productivity effect. They are also influenced however by contrasts in the extent to which the structures of two economies favour high or low productivity (net output per man) activities, the structural, or 'composition' effect. The potential importance of this structural effect is demonstrated by the hypothetical, two sector, two country, model presented in table 3.4.

Table 3.4. *National productivity ratios: a hypothetical example*

	Country I			Country II			
	Labour force	Standardised output	Output per man	Labour force	Standardised output	Output per man	Comparative productivity
Sector A	20	120	6	30	360	12	2·00
Sector B	80	80	1	20	40	2	2·00
Total	100	200	2	50	400	8	4·00

In this case, although comparative country II/country I productivity in both sectors is 2, comparative productivity for the whole industrial economy is 4. The explanation of this apparent paradox lies in the concentration of country I's labour force in sector B, where (absolute) labour productivity is low, and in country II's concentration in the high productivity sector A. The structural effect in this (extreme) case accounts for half the national productivity differential. It is quite possible for comparative sectoral productivity ratios to be unity – with labour productivity in a given activity identical in both countries – whilst national productivity differs significantly owing to structural contrasts in the two economies.

Separating the structural and productivity effects is not as straightforward as might be expected. There is no unique method for making the separation. The ratio 2·63 in table 3.5 measures the US/UK comparative productivity ratio for the industrial economy on the assumption that the sectoral pattern of British output was identical with the United States', each country retaining its own sectoral productivity levels. The difference between this hypothetical ratio, and the actual ratio, a factor of 1·01, is a measure of the structural effect. It suggests that American industrial productivity receives a mere one per cent boost from the economy's relative concentration in high productivity activities. The obverse is that, even if sectoral productivity levels were the same in both countries, British industrial productivity would be a little below the

Table 3.5. *Productivity and structural effects, 1977*

UK = 1·00

	Comparative industrial productivity	Productivity effects		Structural effects	
		British output pattern	Other country output pattern	British output pattern	Other country output pattern
US/UK	2·66	2·58	2·63	1·03	1·01
Germany/UK	1·43	1·45	1·53	0·99	0·93

American level due to the relatively greater weight of low productivity activities.

A slightly different result, suggesting a productivity effect of 2·58 and a structural impact of 1·03, is obtained if the procedure is repeated on the assumption that the American output pattern was identical with the British. The discrepancy reflects the fact that the patterns of sectoral labour productivities, whilst similar, are not identical in the two countries.

Table 3.5 suggests, similarly, that compared with the productivity impact, the structural effect plays but a minor role in shaping the Germany/UK overall industrial productivity ratio. In this case, however, the marginal structural advantage lies with the United Kingdom.

Thus the data in table 3.5 suggest that regardless of which measure is used the structural impact on Britain's comparative industrial productivity is very small. The corollary is that Britain's poor performance is essentially due to low comparative productivity recorded in the individual sectors shown in table 1.1.

Another complication encountered when separating the productivity and structural effects is that – as we shall see in chapter 6 – the results depend on the level at which the separation is conducted. Sectoral productivity ratios themselves will to some extent be shaped by structural factors: comparative sectoral productivity is influenced by differences between two countries in the extent to which high and low productivity activities in sub-sectors feature in the sector's overall make-up. Much of the especially large US/UK extractive industry productivity differential recorded in earlier years was attributable essentially to the comparison of high productivity oil extraction in the United States with low productivity coal mining in the United Kingdom. Indeed, in the final analysis even differences in the product mix within a narrowly specified activity will contribute towards a structural effect.

This said, it seems improbable that the relatively small role which table 3·5 indicates for a structural explanation of Britain's poor performance would be far from the mark. Such a minor impact reflects the essential similarity of the economic structures of the United Kingdom, United States and Germany,[1] and whilst the importance of individual sub-sectors, industries and products may differ significantly between the three countries, the number of such exceptions will be limited so that the structural impact is indeed likely to be small compared with the effect of international differences in productivity levels pure and simple.

It is appropriate at this juncture to pose a further question on which the results throw light. Given the need to produce our current basket of goods, how much larger are British labour inputs than they would be if we enjoyed, sector by sector, the benefit of American or German productivity levels? The answer is that, in this sense, our industry in 1977 was 'overmanned' 2·58 times compared with America's and by 1·45 times compared with Germany's. It can be seen that these ratios are identical with those derived in table 3.5 on the assumption that American and German outputs were distributed on the British pattern but with American and German productivity levels. It should be stressed that such a concept and measure of overmanning is hypothetical and hybrid in nature. By the time that British sectoral productivity levels attained achievements currently recorded in the United States or Germany, both the sectoral pattern of British output and American and German productivity levels would have changed.

Sectoral contributions to industrial productivity differences

Were the overall industrial ratios, 2·66 and 1·43, in table 1.1 weighted averages of the component sectoral ratios for the respective pairs of countries, the extent to which each overall ratio is influenced by a given comparative sectoral productivity differential would be readily determined. The effect would be measured by the size of the difference between the sectoral and the overall ratio, coupled with the sector's weight. However, as previously emphasised, the industrial ratios are not simply weighted averages of the component sectoral ratios. At the risk of repetition, they are derived from absolute sectoral productivity levels, averaged first for each country on the basis of sectoral labour force weights, then compared internationally.

However, there does exist a device which enables us to gauge, if in a somewhat approximate fashion, a sector's impact, in both direction and degree, on the overall comparative industrial productivity ratio. In essence, it consists of calculating a series of international industrial productivity ratios in which the sector in question is accorded its actual performance as measured by the ratios in table 1.1, whilst identical productivity levels – ratios cf 1·00 – are assumed for each of the other five

[1] See table 1.2.

Table 3.6. *Net sectoral contributions to international industrial productivity differences, 1977*

Percentages

	Contribution to the: US/UK differential	Germany/UK differential
Agriculture	5·5	−4·3
Extractive industries	6·9	5·0
Manufacturing	57·4	61·4
Construction	5·5	27·3
Public utilities	7·7	6·7
Transport	17·0	3·9
TOTAL	100·0	100·0

sectors. The results of this exercise are set out in table 3.6 which shows the percentage contribution of each sector to the productivity differentials that have emerged between the United Kingdom and the United States and Germany.

The most striking feature of the table is the size of the manufacturing sector's impact. Though in neither case is the manufacturing productivity ratio much worse than the industrial average (2·91 compared with 2·66 in the US/UK comparison, and 1·52 compared with 1·43 in the Germany/UK comparison), in both it accounts for over half the total effect, reflecting the size of this sector in all three countries. For the rest the construction sector is responsible for much of the discrepancy in the Germany/UK performance, and transport in the US/UK comparison. Other sector impacts tend to be comparatively small; nor do we reap much overall benefit from the superiority of our agriculture to Germany's.

A word of caution needs to be added to this piece of analysis. The results should not be interpreted as an unequivocal allocation between sectors of the blame for our poor performance. For productivity levels achieved in one sector are in some measure a reflection of achievements in another. Improvements in the productivity of air passenger transport are in a large measure due to the ability of manufacturing industry to construct bigger and better airliners. And the improved performance of this latter activity owes much to scientific research conducted in universities – outside the industrial sector altogether. Nevertheless, the contents of tables 1.1 and 3.6 enable us to identify the sectors where international productivity differences immediately manifest themselves.

CHANGES IN PRODUCTIVITY RATIOS

Recent developments

The considerable degree of stability between the 1968 and 1977 patterns of sectoral productivity ratios which table 1.1 reveals in the case of both pairs of country comparisons has already been commented upon. Further interesting features emerge when the ratios are plotted in charts 3.1 and 3.2 for intervening years. One is struck, especially, by the minimal significance of short term, annual, fluctuations in these international productivity ratios. This feature is particularly significant when contrasted with the often pronounced annual instability – recorded in charts 3.3 to 3.8 – in the sectoral output and employment levels from which these ratios are obtained.

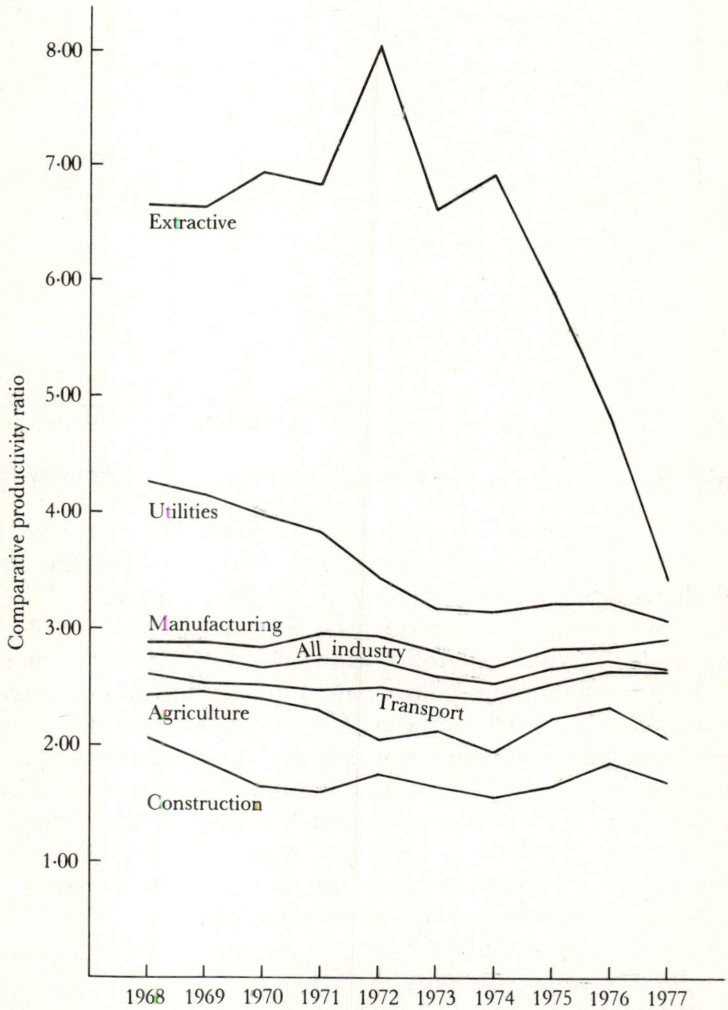

Chart 3.1. Comparative productivity ratios 1968–77: US/UK

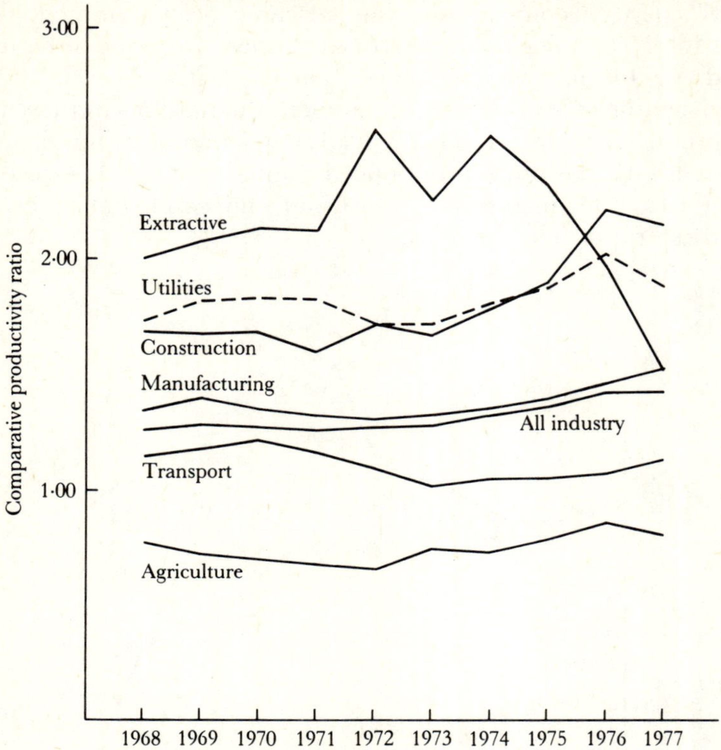

Chart 3.2. Comparative productivity ratios 1968–77: Germany/UK

This stability derives from two sources. At the national level there is, hardly surprisingly, a considerable association between the *direction* of annual changes in sectoral outputs and employment, even if the sizes of the respective movements are often far from proportionate. As a result the amplitude of annual fluctuations in labour productivity changes can be much less than in the component output and labour force series. Secondly, there is much inter-country similarity in the nature and timing of short-term variations in sectoral productivity levels, further dampening instability in international comparative productivity ratios. Again this effect is hardly unexpected. Because of their close ties the three economies normally experience cyclical output fluctuations at much the same times. For instance – and in particular – chart 3.5 reveals similar basic manufacturing output changes over the years in the three countries, especially the dip between 1973 and 1975 and a concomitant pause in long term productivity growth.

This systematic dampening of short term fluctuations facilitates the interpretation of our results in two important ways. First, to all intents

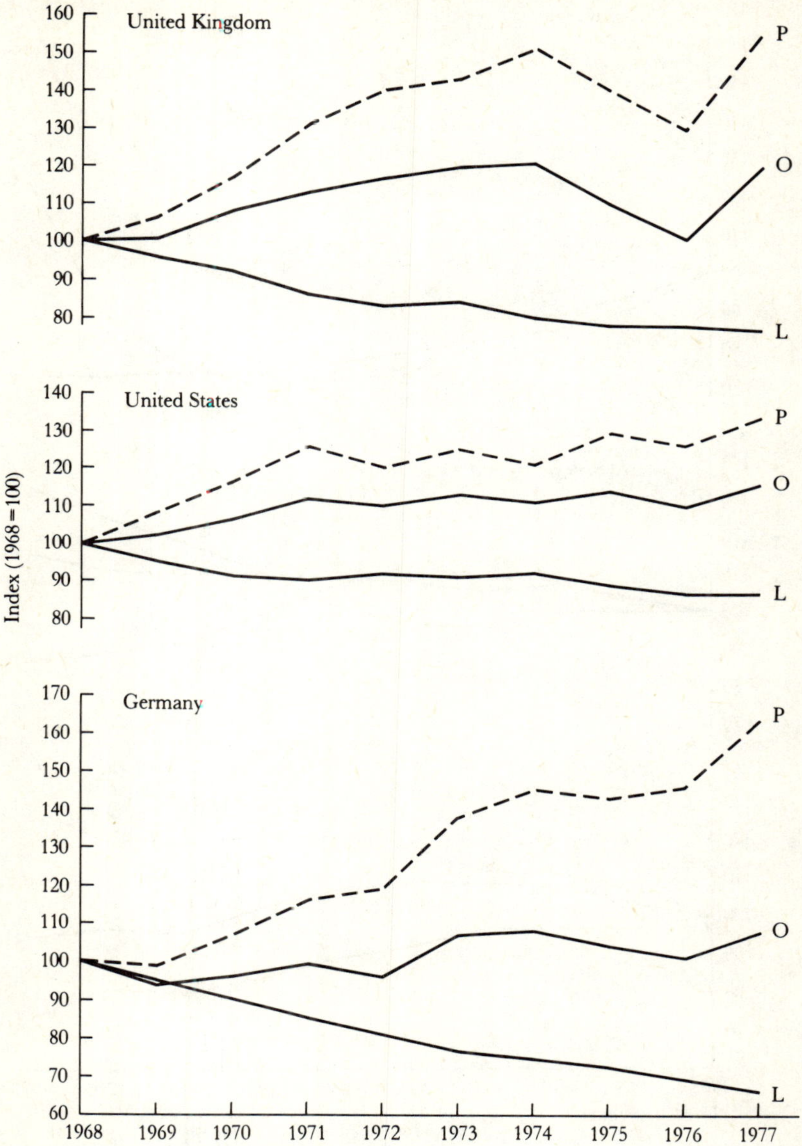

Notes: P = productivity index
O = output index
L = labour force index

Chart 3.3. Output, employment and productivity changes, 1968–77: Agriculture

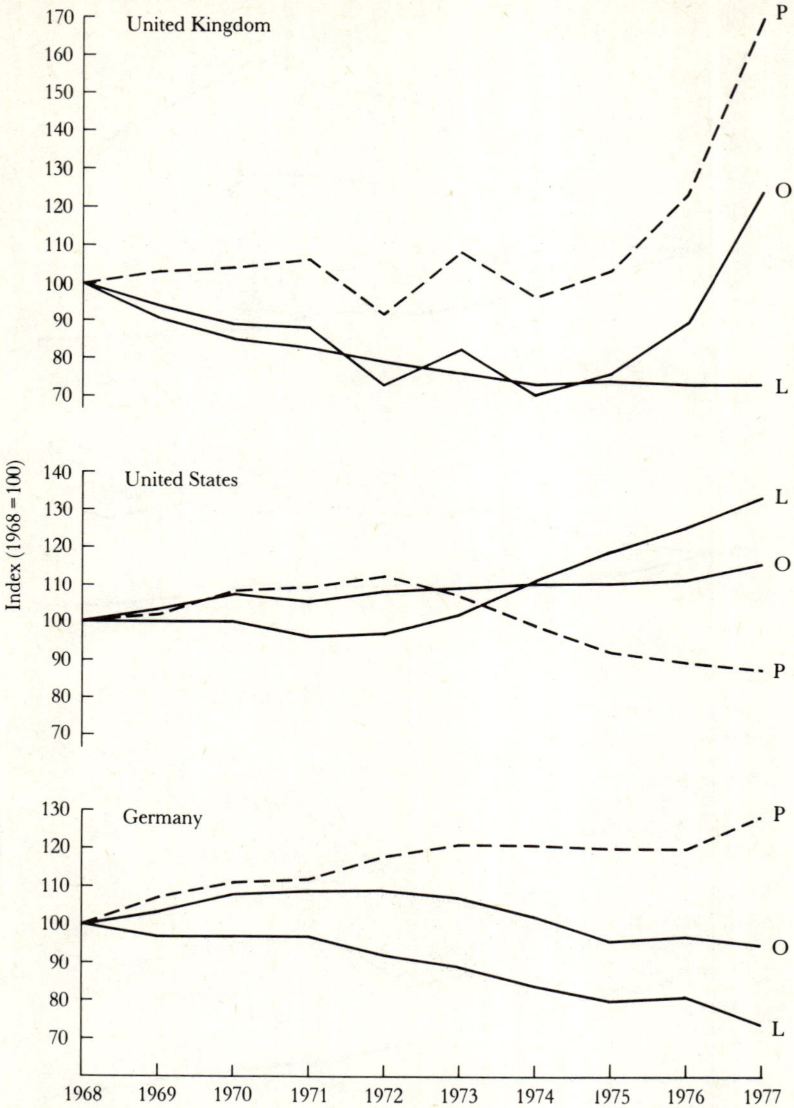

Notes: see chart 3.3

Chart 3.4. Output, employment and productivity changes, 1968–77: Extractive industries

and purposes it obviates the need to identify for each sector, in each country, the year when short term conditions (including capacity utilisation) are such that a labour productivity figure obtains which can be regarded as the best, in terms of currently available performance, for

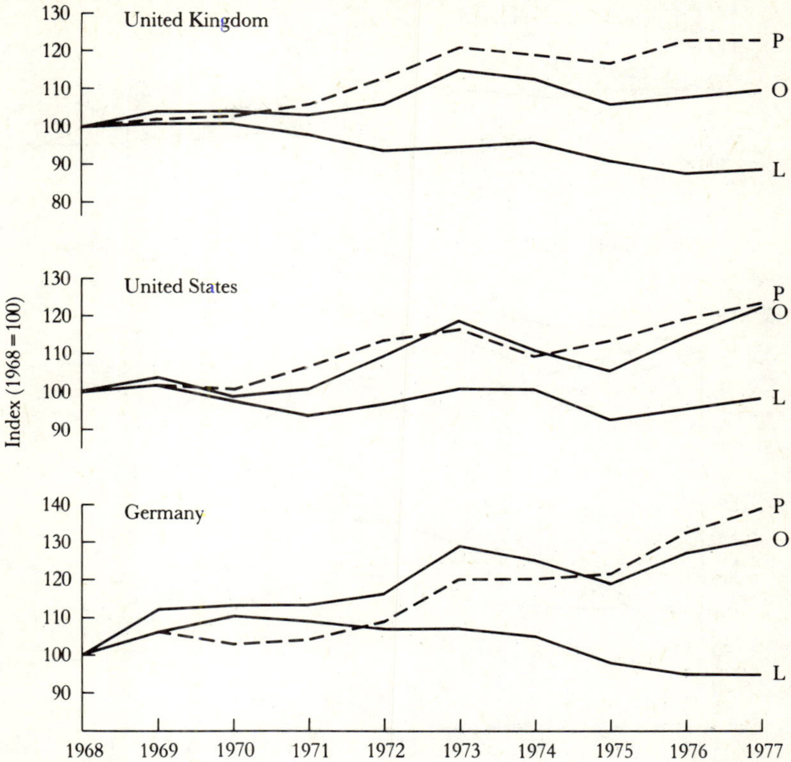

Notes: see chart 3.3

Chart 3.5. Output, employment and productivity changes, 1968–77: Manufacturing

that sector and for the international comparison. Put another way, the patterns of comparative productivity ratios are little affected if, regardless of year, the highest sectoral productivity levels recently attained are compared between countries.

The principal exceptions are the extractive industries and construction. In the former case the significantly different ratios which would emerge comparing productivity levels for different years would reflect not short-term fluctuations in economic conditions and capacity utilisation but longer-term changes in the development cycle for oil extraction, especially a switch to exploration in the United States at a time when British production came on stream. In the case of construction maximum American productivity was actually attained in 1968, British in 1971 and German in 1977. Comparing these optimum productivity levels yields a US/UK ratio of 1·72 (compared with 1·70 in 1977) and a German ratio of 1·87 (compared with 2·18 in 1977).

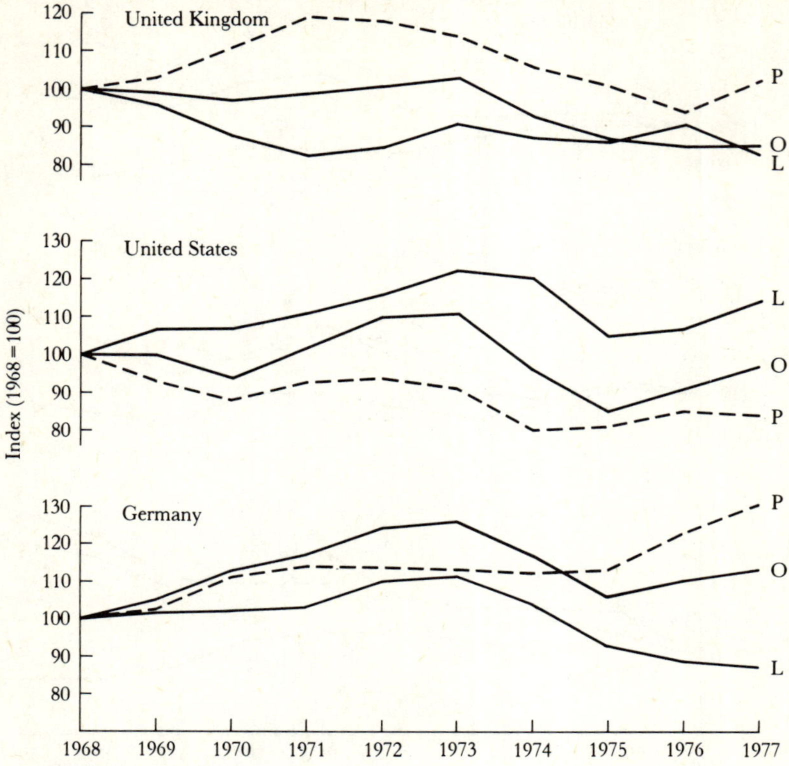

Notes: see chart 3.3

Chart 3.6. Output, employment and productivity changes, 1968–77: Construction

Secondly, comparative stability in these ratios over the short term means that longer term trends are readily evident. Examining these trends for the US/UK comparison in table 1.1 and charts 3.1 to 3.8, it can be seen that there has been little change in the relative performance of the British manufacturing and transportation sectors, some tendency to improve in construction and agriculture, and more spectacular longer-term gains in the comparative performance of our public utilities and extractive industries.

Visually the quite dramatic way in which US/UK comparative productivity in extractive activities has improved over this period appears to dominate the picture. It is the one sector where, instead of fairly stable comparative productivity, or a tendency towards continuous gradual improvement in Britain's comparative performance over the period, there was a sudden and dramatic improvement starting in the mid seventies, from very high ratios in the early years, 6·68 in 1968

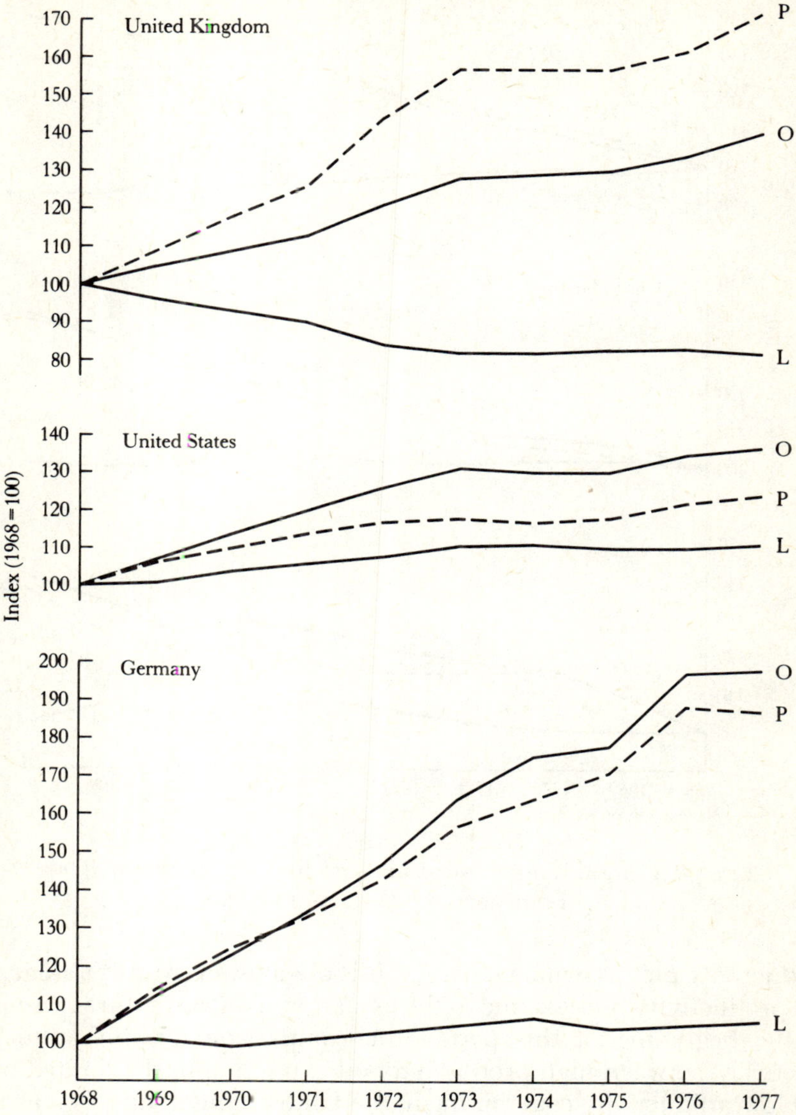

Notes: see chart 3.3

Chart 3.7. Output, employment and productivity changes, 1968–77: Utilities

and 8·06 in 1972,[1] down to a ratio of 3·42 by 1977. Although the purpose of this chapter is to portray rather than explain the comparative

[1] The peaks, 1972 and 1974, of Britain's worst performance in this sector are traceable to essentially transient factors: coal production lost as a result of strikes.

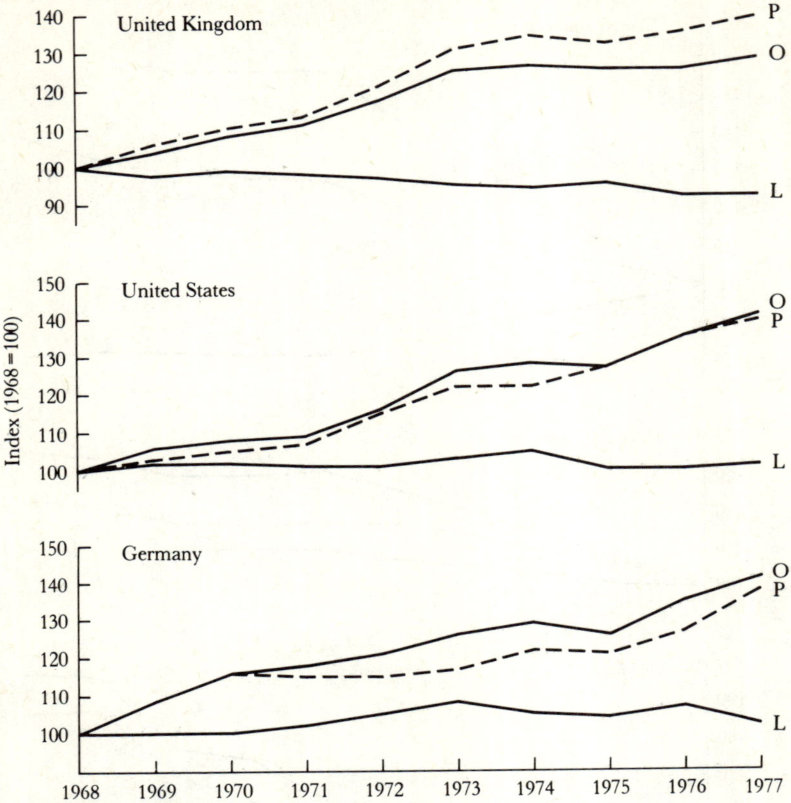

Notes: see chart 3.3

Chart 3.8. Output, employment and productivity changes, 1968–77: Transport and Communications

productivity picture which emerges, it is obvious, even at this stage, that this productivity boost is due to the exploitation of our natural resources. At the beginning of this period the comparison for this sector was effectively between high productivity oil extraction in the United States and low productivity coal mining in the United Kingdom; it is now more like with like.

It might seem surprising that this sharp productivity improvement has not done more to improve our overall industrial productivity in comparison with the US. It should be appreciated in this context that the series cease in 1977 so that later gains in extractive activities are not recorded. But the principal explanation as to why comparative British industrial productivity does not reflect to a greater extent the improvements in our performance in individual sectors resides in their weights;

those registering the more significant gains, the extractive sector and public utilities being the smallest, whilst comparative US/UK productivity in manufacturing, by far the largest sector, changed little between 1968 and 1977.

There has been a gradual deterioration in British industrial performance compared with that of Germany, from a ratio of 1·26 in 1968 to 1·43 in 1977. Looking at the component sectors, there seems to have been little change in our comparative performance in agriculture and transport, but some deterioration in public utilities and more especially, construction. More significant, in view of its weight, there has been a fairly continuous deterioration in the comparative performance of British manufacturing. Again, the bright spot is in the extractive industry sector where a very significant improvement was registered, from a ratio of 2 in 1968 to about $1\frac{1}{2}$ in 1977.

Long-term changes: an Anglo-American comparison

We take the opportunity which our data afford to make long term comparisons, over a series of decades, of sectoral productivity ratios for the United Kingdom and the United States. It might appear that such comparisons can be made simply by taking back our measures of sectoral productivities using appropriate labour productivity indices. For both theoretical and practical reasons, however, this method is unsuitable when tracing changes over a large number of years. In the first place attempts to measure labour force changes are bedevilled with alterations to the statistical bases and in sectoral definitions. But more especially, when real output indices are stretched over long periods of time their reliability may suffer greatly due to changes in a sector's industrial structure and output composition in the face of which attempts to re-base the relevant indices, using changing weights, are somewhat less than satisfactory. Even when use of this approach is restricted, as in the present study, to a comparatively short run of years (1968 to 1977), its effectiveness is strained in those activities, such as the extractive industries, where the period in question witnessed substantial structural adjustments.[1]

A more satisfactory approach to such long-term comparisons is to compare productivity results obtained by direct measurement in a series

[1] A comparison was made between the sectoral ratios obtained by Paige and Bombach (*A Comparison of National Output*) for 1950 and estimates for the same year based on our 1968 results taken back by appropriate output and labour force indices. Whilst the revealed discrepancies, at least in terms of rankings of sectoral ratios, were not too alarming (transport apart) the exercise confirmed that this approach is unsatisfactory for gauging long-term changes in productivity ratios. In particular the 1950 ratio for the extractive industries – where structural changes have been exceptionally important – emerges as 3·98 when 'taken back' from 1968, compared with the Paige and Bombach ratio of 7·69.

Table 3.7. *Long-term changes in comparative productivity: US/UK*

UK = 1·00

	1935–9 Rostas	1950 Paige and Bombach	1968 Present study	1977 Present study
Agriculture	1·03	2·22	2·42	2·09
Extractive & utilities	3·60	7·69	5·17	3·23
Extractive	4·15		6·68	3·42
Utilities	1·80		4·26	3·06
Manufacturing	2·15	2·92	2·89	2·91
Construction	1·15	1·50	2·06	1·70
All transport	2·80[a]	4·12	2·62	2·64
Transport	2·85[b]	4·58[c]	2·40	2·13
Communications	2·70	2·64	2·84	3·34
All industry	1·81	2·99	2·78	2·66

Sources: Rostas, *Comparative Productivity*, especially chapter VI; Paige and Bombach, *A Comparison of National Output*, especially chapter IV.

[a] Estimated.

[b] From a range of 2·70 to 3·00

[c] On UK prices; US price result is 2·55

of widely dispersed years. Thanks to the pioneering work of early researchers in this field, such an approach is feasible. Table 3.7 sets out, in as comparable a form as possible, the comparative US/UK sectoral labour productivity ratios derived respectively by Rostas for 1935–39 and by Paige and Bombach for 1950,[1] and compares them with the results obtained in the present study for 1968 and 1977. For each of the four periods an 'industrial' productivity ratio has been calculated using an aggregation methodology comparable to that specified in chapter 2.

The developments portrayed in table 3.7 should be treated with some caution since the results are not wholly comparable. Not only have there been improvements over these four decades in the statistical data, but also the measurement methods used in the three projects differ in certain significant respects. For instance, Rostas's result for manufacturing is based on a selection of industries which accounted for no more than a half of British manufacturing net output and about two thirds of American: the present study covers the entire sector. And unlike the present study, Paige and Bombach sought, by double deflation and other techniques, to adjust their results for variations in inputs of raw materials, etc. In all three studies, the construction industry ratio, especially, is subject to a considerable margin of error: Paige and Bombach believing that the ratio was 'substantially above 120 per cent and substantially below 200 per cent' accordingly used 'an index of 150 per cent for computational purposes'.[2]

[1] *Op. cit.*

[2] *A Comparison of National Output*, p. 214.

This said, in all three studies the measurement methodologies were broadly similar. It is especially striking, therefore, that table 3.7 suggests a high degree of stability over time in the sectoral pattern of comparative productivity ratios, a stability already commented on for more recent periods. For long periods, too, the British bright spots have been agriculture and construction – in the latter case even when due allowance is made for a considerable margin of error. The laggards have been the extractive industries and public utilities.

Between lie the manufacturing and transport sectors. The productivity ratio for the former appears to have differed little from the average during the middle years but in both the late thirties and late seventies was perceptibly worse. Given the importance of manufacturing in the industrial economy, it would be wrong to underestimate the extent to which, at such times, manufacturing has been responsible for Britain's poor performance.

Two factors need to be borne in mind when considering the transport sector. First, whenever there is a choice, ratios based on British price weights have been used in table 3.7. This choice is especially relevant in the case of transport, particularly in earlier decades when railways (and the contrast in UK/US freight/passenger activities and prices) were more important. Had results based on American weights been taken from Paige and Bombach, the transport ratio would have been 2·55 not 4·58 (and for the whole transport and communications sector 2·52 not 4·12). Secondly, whilst distance travelled is in principle accommodated in all three studies – favouring the United States – only in the later results (1968 and 1977) has a systematic attempt been made to allow for the 'terminal work element' which, to some extent, redresses the balance to the United Kingdom. This may help explain why British performance in this sector seems comparatively poor in the early part of the period, comparatively good more recently. Communications, like manufacturing, show up especially badly in the late 1930s and late 1970s.

Moving from stability of the sectoral patterns to trends over time, caution must be exercised in the interpretation. It seems fairly clear, however, that after a sharp deterioration in the 1940s there may have been some slight improvement in comparative British industrial performance in recent decades.

The earlier deterioration reflected, in part, a continuation of historical trends. For instance, Rostas shows that in both manufacturing and agriculture labour productivity had been rising significantly faster in the United States than in the United Kingdom for most of the early part of this century.[1] Secondly, certain structural changes in the American

[1] *Comparative Productivity*, pp. 42 and 79.

economy did much to boost overall productivity in the earlier period. There was a significant switch from low productivity coal mining to high productivity gas and oil, and by 1950 American employment in (low productivity) agriculture represented no more than 12 per cent of the economy's labour force, compared with 19 per cent in the late 1930s. But the extent to which the improvement in American performance in these years was experienced in virtually all industrial sectors points to the influence of a much more general factor: the extent to which, compared with Britain, the American economy benefited from wartime and postwar conditions in terms of growth, investment and productivity.

Responsibility for the improvement during recent decades in Britain's comparative performance is to be found mainly in developments in the extractive industries and public utilities. Little is traceable to manufacturing. The role of the transport sector in this improvement is more difficult to discern, but there has certainly been a switch away from activities where the US/UK productivity differential is large (railways and ports) towards those where it is smaller (road haulage and air transport).

4

GENERAL INFLUENCES ON COMPARATIVE INDUSTRIAL PERFORMANCE

It is plain that in a multi-sectoral study such as this only proximate causes of international productivity differences can be investigated. We could not pretend to trace in any detail the influence and impact on productivity differentials of the plethora of factors, general and specific, physical, historical, institutional and economic, which determine the comparative productivity ratios that have been measured. Such an exhaustive enquiry would require at least one book per sector. At best it is possible to focus attention on the more likely influences, an approach which in turn may point to promising avenues of future research. The analysis is also subject to other constraints.

Typically studies of inter-country differences in labour productivity have concentrated on measuring and explaining contrasts in the performance of the manufacturing sector.[1] Such exercises have usually relied upon econometric analyses of selected manufacturing activities and have been directed to such explanatory variables as size of markets, size of establishment, degree of integration, capital intensity, industrial relations and quality of labour force.

This line is followed in chapter 6. The expectations if such an approach were adopted would be rather different when attention is directed, as in this chapter, to the whole of the industrial sector, to activities as diverse as agriculture and transport. For instance, whilst different manufacturing activities are sufficiently akin for the concept of establishment (or factory) to apply to all, little common meaning could be attached to the same concept in the case of construction activities and transport services. Any attempt to discover whether, as is the case among certain manufacturing activities, productivity varies systematically with size of establishment, would have little meaning in the context of the industrial sector broadly defined.

Nor is the basic form of the production function likely to be the same for each industrial sector. Whilst the parameters of the function appropriate for different manufacturing activities may vary significantly, it is legitimate to assume that the function itself will be essentially the

[1] See chapter 2.

same, say the Cobb-Douglas formulation:

$$Y = aL^kC^j$$

where

$$Y = \text{output},\ L = \text{units of labour},\ C = \text{units of capital.}$$

Yet such a production function, neglecting as it does the amount of land used, would be highly inappropriate for agriculture. Ratios of land per worker are highly relevant to international contrasts in agricultural productivity but perhaps of comparatively little consequence in most of the other activities we have considered. Other factors, such as those associated with environmental contrasts, will also exert specific effects on productivity levels in particular sectors.

In general, therefore, there is much less reason to anticipate that a series of common factors, such as those normally considered in the context of manufacturing, would serve to explain international differences in labour productivity in other sectors. As much as in explanatory variables of this general kind the causes of sectoral productivity differences must be sought in factors which, in all likelihood, are special and particular to a given activity. In the following chapter, attention is turned to such considerations.

These warnings do not preclude the examination, as possible causal influences, of factors which are conventionally regarded as candidates for explaining international productivity differences in manufacturing. Where it is theoretically reasonable, and statistically practicable, there is justification for ascertaining whether such factors are systematically associated with labour productivity differentials. It should be emphasised however that the relevant tests, given that we are concerned with six sectors only, cannot be as rigorous as those which are possible with a large number of manufacturing industries. This means, in particular, that we must be content with relatively unsophisticated tests of association and are in no position to estimate any given factor's likely net impact on productivity – a procedure which is possible when multiple regression techniques are applied to a large number of industries and explanatory variables.

In the search for factors which might be systematically associated with, and exert an influence on, international sectoral productivity differences, we have been guided by two principles, the identification of possible independent variables which theoretically might be expected to play an important role, and a selection from these of those which are measurable in each country on a common and convenient basis for the six sectors. Application of these criteria pinpoints the following factors: absolute labour productivity levels; capital intensity; size of markets;

quality of labour force; and industrial relations. A somewhat different kind of variable has also been taken into account: sectoral rates of output growth. A number of studies have focussed attention on essentially static considerations of the kind noted above. Other exercises have pointed to the role which differential changes in manufacturing outputs also play in shaping rates of growth of manufacturing productivity. By considering both types of influence the present chapter seeks not merely to extend conventional analysis from manufacturing to other industrial activities but also to proceed some way towards integrating possible static and dynamic explanations.

ABSOLUTE AND COMPARATIVE LABOUR PRODUCTIVITY

Should the data reveal a common sectoral pattern of net output per man between the three countries then it would be logical to enquire whether an association exists between this pattern of absolute labour productivities and Britain's comparative performance as measured by the sectoral labour productivity ratios. It is perhaps easier to apply this test than to interpret the results. In effect, however, one is asking whether Britain is comparatively effective in those activities where, for whatever reason, there appears to be greater scope for high labour productivity; or whether our performance is best in sectors where, in all three countries, absolute productivity levels are low. The test has meaning and can be applied only if a reasonably common sectoral pattern of labour productivity is found in each country.

Table 4.1. *Sectoral labour productivity levels, 1977*

£ per man

	United Kingdom	United States	Germany
Public utilities	11900	36533	22491
Extractive industries	10929	37377	16503
Transport	6777	17891	7726
Agriculture	4997	10444	4098
Manufacturing	4866	14160	7396
Construction	4799	8158	10462
All industry	5488	14604	7856

Table 4.1 shows, in £ of net output per man, the absolute productivity levels measured in 1977 for each of the six sectors for each of the three countries. They have been ranked in order of British productivity levels,[1]

[1] Since the measure has further uses and because conceptually it is more appropriate, these productivity levels are those measured in £ sterling obtained by the reverse valuation technique explained in chapter 2. A picture, for each country, of the pattern of sectoral labour productivities based on *per capita* contribution to GDP, valued in domestic currencies, yields results which are not too dissimilar, though in the case of Germany extractive industries fall down the list and manufacturing moves up.

from highest to lowest – public utilities, extractive industries, transport, agriculture, manufacturing and construction. The first point to note is that there is considerably less dispersion in the British sectoral performance than in the case of the United States or Germany. In the United Kingdom the highest sectoral labour productivity level is no more than some 2½ times the lowest; in the United States and Germany the corresponding factors are respectively about 4½ and 5½.

As to the sectoral pattern, the principal departures from a common picture are the relatively high productivity recorded in German construction and relatively low productivity in German agriculture. Otherwise the country rankings are not too dissimilar. This is especially so if the positions of British agriculture and manufacturing were interchanged – and it should be appreciated that the productivity difference between these two is small in relation to the likely margin of error. Thus, although there is no unique sectoral pattern in the three countries, something of a common pattern may be discerned in that public utilities and extractive industries tend to be high productivity sectors in all three countries, whilst transport, manufacturing, construction and agriculture are low productivity activities.

Table 4.2. *Absolute and comparative labour productivity levels, 1977*

	Comparative productivity ratios, UK = 1·00	
	US/UK	Germany/UK
High productivity sectors		
Public utilities	3·07	1·89
Extractive industries	3·42	1·51
Low productivity sectors		
Transport	2·64	1·14
Manufacturing	2·91	1·52
Construction	1·70	2·18
Agriculture	2·09	0·82

Table 4.2 suggests that for the US/UK comparison there is some association between our comparative performance and these absolute productivity levels, the United Kingdom being especially bad in high productivity sectors, comparatively better in low productivity activities.

In the Germany/UK comparison the results are less clear cut.[1] But if the maverick, construction, ratio is left out of account then all that remains to qualify the same generalisation (of poor British performance in high productivity activities, good performance in low ones) is a Germany/UK manufacturing ratio akin to that in extractive industries.[2]

[1] Taking the British pattern of productivity levels, a correlation coefficient with patterns of productivity differentials is +0·75 in the US/UK comparison and +0·23 in the Germany/UK comparison.

[2] Prior to 1977 the Germany/UK ratio for extractive industries was comfortably in excess of that for manufacturing.

This blurring of the Germany/UK relationship compared with fairly clear cut US/UK patterns also characterises some of the later results. A possible explanation – which receives some verification – is that the Germany/UK sectoral productivity differentials, in contrast to US/UK differentials, are small in relation to the measurement errors involved.

These results, coupled with the observation that the range of sectoral productivity levels in the UK is lower than in the US or Germany, suggest that Britain has failed, especially, to achieve high productivity levels in those activities where the productivity potential is greatest.

COMPARATIVE PRODUCTIVITY AND CAPITAL INTENSITY

Any consideration of factors giving rise to international productivity differences must embrace if at all possible the degree of intensity of capital per worker. Two distinct hypotheses can be tested: that Britain's comparative performance is worse in capital intensive activities; and/or that the sectoral pattern of inter-country comparative productivity ratios is correlated with the sectoral pattern of inter-country capital intensity ratios. The first hypothesis is analogous to the analysis of the previous section in which the relationship between the sectoral pattern of comparative productivity ratios and the pattern of absolute productivity levels was considered. It tests the supposition that the more capital intensive an operation, the greater the scope for higher labour productivity and for wider productivity differentials. It is however distinct from the earlier test in that inter-sectoral variations in capital intensity are but one influence (together with natural resource endowments for example) on inter-sectoral differences in labour productivity levels so that, within a given country, the pattern of sectors ranked by capital intensity need not align with their pattern of labour productivity.

The first hypothesis is applicable only if the sectoral patterns of capital intensities are basically similar in the three countries. Table 4.3 suggests that there is, indeed, much similarity in these patterns.[1] In the United Kingdom and United States capital intensity is highest in public utilities, followed in both countries by transport, extractive industries, agriculture, manufacturing, and finally construction. Reversing the positions of extractive industries and agriculture the same ranking also applies to Germany.[2]

[1] Based on 1973 gross capital stock data. The choice of this year was effectively determined by the latest series of sectoral capital stock data available for the United States: estimates presented in J. W. Kendrick, K. S. Lee, J. Lomask, *The National Wealth of the United States, by Major Sector and Industry*, The Conference Board, New York, 1976. Official capital stock estimates for the UK are taken from *National Income and Expenditure* and for Germany from the *Statistisches Jahrbuch*.

[2] Comparisons between the US/UK, Germany/UK and US/Germany patterns in table 4.3 yield in all cases correlation coefficients approaching unity.

Table 4.3. *Capital intensity[a] and comparative productivity, 1973*

	Capital intensity			Comparative productivity ratios (UK = 1·00)	
	United Kingdom[b] (£ per man)	United States[b] ($ per man)	Germany[c] (DM per man)	US/UK	Germany/UK
Agriculture	8126	32704	69090	2·11	0·75
Extractive industries	9560	66066	59952	6·64	2·25
Manufacturing	7657	17340	52720	2·80	1·34
Construction	1865	7073	19409	1·65	1·70
Public utilities	74707	264234	578475	3·19	1·73
Transport	21541	87689	141564	2·43	1·02
All industry	10447	34102	66148	2·59	1·29

Sources: OECD, *Labour Force Statistics*; UK, *National Income and Expenditure*; US, Kendrick *et al.*, *The National Wealth of the United States, op. cit.*; Germany, *Statistisches Jahrbuch.*

[a] Gross capital stock per man

[b] At 1973 prices

[c] At 1970 prices

It is instructive to compare this international pattern of sectoral capital intensities with that observed in the previous section for absolute sectoral productivity levels. In both series, public utilities are ranked highest, and manufacturing, agriculture and construction feature at the bottom of the scale, whilst transport ranks higher on capital intensity than on productivity levels. There is less association between the patterns of comparative productivity ratios and capital intensity than between the productivity ratios and absolute productivity levels.

Table 4.4 presents the data required for testing the second capital intensity possibility. This hypothesis postulates that the sectoral pattern of comparative productivity ratios is (positively) associated with the sectoral pattern of international differences in capital per man: that the sector displaying the largest inter-country difference in capital intensity will also yield the largest comparative productivity ratio. For this test, American and German capital stock data were standardised in £ sterling in order to compare capital per man between countries. In view of the nature of the capital stock estimates, and the procedures used for converting domestic currency valuations to £ sterling,[1] it would be

[1] United States and German capital stock data valued in domestic currencies were converted to £ sterling using Kravis (*op. cit.*) price indices. The US/UK 1973 index, 2·80, was that implied in the standardised Kravis gross capital formation series. The corresponding Germany/UK price index, applied to the 1970 German capital data was 9·45. Because the asset structure by sector is not always known, it was necessary to deflate the capital stock data in each activity by these common ratios. A sensitivity analysis applied to American data, using as weights British capital formation figures by asset and sector, yielded a series of US/UK capital stock price indices which varied between sector and the following capital intensive ratios (those actually used in table 4.4 in brackets): agriculture 1·46 (1·44); extractive industries 2·37 (2·47); manufacturing 0·93 (0·81);

Table 4.4. *Comparative capital intensity and productivity ratios*

	Capital intensity (£ per man)		Capital intensity ratio	Comparative productivity ratio UK = 1·00
	United Kingdom[a]	United States		
US/UK 1973				
Agriculture	8126	11680	1·44	2·11
Extractive industries	9560	23595	2·47	6·64
Manufacturing	7657	6193	0·81	2·80
Construction	1865	2526	1·35	1·65
Public utilities	74707	94369	1·26	3·19
Transport	21541	31317	1·45	2·43
All industry	10447	12179	1·17	2·59
Germany/UK 1970	United Kingdom	Germany		
Agriculture	4987	6036	1·21	0·70
Extractive industries	5645	8190	1·45	2·13
Manufacturing	4930	4240	0·86	1·35
Construction	1389	1896	1·37	1·71
Public utilities	51624	59848	1·16	1·84
Transport	14631	13159	0·90	1·21
All industry	6945	7475	1·08	1·28

Sources: See table 4.3 and text.

[a] Note UK 1973 data for comparison with US is valued in 1973 prices, UK 1970 data for comparison with Germany is valued in 1970 prices.

unwise to attach undue reliability to the resulting capital intensity data. For instance, it is hard to believe that capital intensity in British manufacturing is greater than in the United States.

There is some evidence of a positive association between the two ratio series in the country comparison of table 4.4. In both pairs of comparisons the capital intensity differentials, like the comparative productivity ratios, were highest in the extractive industries,[2] so that Britain's poor (but much improved) performance in this activity may be explained, in part, by under-capitalisation. On the other hand, in the second activity where our performance is especially poor, public utilities, the capital intensity differentials differ little from the average of all industrial activities, 1·26 compared with 1·17 in the US/UK comparison, and 1·16 compared with 1·08 in the Germany/UK comparison. At the other end

construction 1·61 (1·35); public utilities 1·35 (1·26); and transport 1·74 (1·45). A comparable sensitivity analysis applied to the 'all industry' data suggests a US/UK capital intensity ratio of 1·28 compared with 1·17 in table 4.4.

[2] This contributes much to a high positive correlation coefficient of +0·80 between the US/UK comparative productivity ratios and comparative capital intensity ratios. The coefficients in the case of the Germany/UK and US/Germany comparison are +0·50 and +0·56 respectively.

of the scale our commendable performance in agriculture appears to materialise despite comparative under-capitalisation.

Finally, it would be wrong to ignore the indication in table 4.4 that in nine of the twelve inter-country sectoral comparisons the British activity appears to be comparatively under-capitalised: manufacturing is the principal, and somewhat surprising, exception.

COMPARATIVE PRODUCTIVITY AND MARKET SIZE

Studies of manufacturing industry have suggested that there may be a positive association between market size and international productivity ratios.[1] The possible existence of such a relationship can be bolstered by theoretical considerations, not least of which are the potential degree of specialisation and economies of scale which larger markets offer.[2] Table 4.5 compares productivity ratios and relative market size among the six sectors: the relative size of sectoral shares of industrial output (based on contribution to GDP) having been used as an indicator of relative market size. Table 4.5 reveals that for the US/UK comparison the most pronounced structural difference lies in the comparatively large American agriculture output, and for the Germany/UK comparison, in the scale of British extractive industries.

Table 4.5. *Relative market size, 1976–7*

	Sectoral share of industrial output			Relative market size	
	UK 1977	US 1977	Germany 1976	US/UK (UK = 1·00)	Germany/UK (UK = 1·00)
Agriculture	5·3	6·4	5·1	1·21	0·96
Extractive industries	5·6	6·2	2·3	1·11	0·41
Manufacturing	54·3	56·1	65·0	1·03	1·20
Construction	12·4	10·5	12·4	0·85	1·00
Public utilities	6·6	5·8	4·9	0·88	0·74
Transport	15·8	14·9	10.3	0·94	0·65
All industry	100·0	100·0	100·0		

Source: Table 1.2.

It is difficult to detect any systematic influence of size on the basis of this test.[3] Agriculture, especially, behaves in a perverse way. If the basic thesis were valid, comparative British-American productivity would be

[1] See, for instance, Frankel, *British and American Manufacturing Productivity*.

[2] Size of production unit is of course also relevant. No generalized associated test, across all six sectors, is possible in the case of size of production unit, since, as already pointed out, a reasonably uniform concept of 'establishment' is difficult to apply to all sectors.

[3] Correlation coefficients between relative market sizes and comparative productivity for the US/UK, Germany/UK and US/Germany comparisons are respectively +0·15, +0·09 and +0·50.

especially low, whereas in fact British agriculture is one of our best sectoral performers *vis-à-vis* the United States; and on the basis of the relative Germany/UK scale of agricultural output we would not anticipate an especially brilliant British agricultural performance whilst in fact it emerges as the best sector in the Germany/UK comparison.

COMPARATIVE PRODUCTIVITY AND LABOUR FORCE QUALITY

It is conventional to emphasise that labour productivity achievements, and differences therein, are influenced and can be explained by a wide variety of factors, capital intensities, scale of output, quality of management, etc. It should not be overlooked however that the efficiency and quality of the labour force itself may contribute significantly to labour productivity performances. In principle we have allowed in our labour productivity comparisons only for variations in the quantity of labour input: for the number of man/woman years of labour in each sector and country.[1] No allowance has been made for international differences in sectoral labour force composition: the male/female structure of a force, its age composition, occupational make-up or skill balance. The effects of all these characteristics on output levels are included in the measured productivity levels and ratios.

A thorough evaluation of the impact of such labour force characteristics on sectoral outputs and labour productivity levels would require a much more extensive analysis than is possible here. In the circumstances reliance is perforce placed on a single statistic which, with certain simplifying assumptions, might be regarded as a surrogate indicator of comparative labour force quality: the (relative) ratio between countries of average compensation per employee in a given sector.

In each sector compensation per employee is an average of wage rates paid to each category of worker – classified by skill, occupation, sex etc. – weighted by the numbers in each group. If it is assumed that distortions in a country's labour market are not such that the remunerations of different kinds of labour are greatly removed from their (marginal) contributions to output, inter-country comparisons of average remuneration can be regarded as approximate indicators of the relative[2] labour force quality in the sectors in question. The results are presented for 1976 in table 4.5.[3]

[1] Apart from an overall adjustment for hours worked in chapter 3.

[2] The measures are standardised (to allow for the fact that average remuneration is expressed in domestic currencies) as relatives of the average sectoral ratio for each pair of countries.

[3] Due to lack of data, no assessment can be made, on this basis, of relative labour force quality in agriculture in the US/UK comparison and in public utilities for the Germany/UK comparison.

Table 4.6. *Comparative productivity and labour force quality, 1976*

	Agriculture	Extractive industries	Manu-facturing	Construction	Public utilities	Transport
Average compensation per employee:						
United Kingdom (£)	2567	4161	3512	3726	4257	4485
United States ($)	. .	19201	15041	15392	18769	17582
Germany (DM)	22851	49857	31083	23311	. .	31355
US/UK comparison (UK = 1·00):						
Comparative labour quality[a]	. .	1·08	1·00	0·97	1·03	0·92
Comparative productivity ratio		4·84	2·84	1·85	3·22	2·63
Germany/UK comparison (UK = 1·00):						
Comparative labour quality[a]	1·04	1·39	1·03	0·73	. .	0·81
Comparative productivity ratio	0·86	1·97	1·47	2·24		1·08

Sources: United Nations, *Yearbook of National Accounts Statistics*; OECD, *Labour Force Statistics.*
[a] Derived from ratios of average compensation, with average sectoral ratio = 1·00

In the case of the US/UK comparison, the results are quite rewarding, suggesting considerable correlation between sectoral patterns of comparative productivity and comparative labour force quality.[1] The United States labour force emerges as relatively the most superior, or least inferior, in extractive industries where its productivity performance is also best compared with the United Kingdom; second are public utilities, whether ranked by relative labour force quality or by productivity; and third, again on both criteria, is manufacturing. At the other end of the scale America's better productivity performance is least marked in construction and transport, where the indicators suggest any relative labour force advantage is also least pronounced.

On the face of it no such relationship can be discerned in the Germany/UK comparison.[2] In particular, in construction, where German productivity is highest relative to the United Kingdom, the relative quality of the German labour force, measured in this fashion, would seem to be lowest. However, it is by no means impossible that the wage rates paid to 'guest workers', who feature largely in the German construction labour force, may unduly distort the comparative labour

[1] The coefficient being +0·82.
[2] The correlation coefficient being +0·06.

force quality indicator for this sector. Indeed, there are grounds for believing that, in terms of effort and application and the amount of labour derived per worker, the quality of this, perhaps compliant labour force, is especially high.[1]

COMPARATIVE PRODUCTIVITY AND STRIKE ACTION

Another test in this series for potential associations concerns the extent of comparative strike action as measured by the relative number of days lost per member of the sector's labour force. Table 4.7 sets out the requisite data, which are unavailable for Germany,[2] so that the test is restricted to the US/UK comparison and then not for years beyond the mid-seventies. To reduce any distortion attributable to untypically prolonged strife in a given year, the numbers of days lost have been averaged over the three years, 1973 to 1975, before being expressed as a ratio of the 1974 labour force.

Table 4.7. *Comparative productivity and strike action, US/UK, 1974*

	Agriculture	Extractive industries	Manu-facturing	Con-struction	Utilities and transport	All industry
Days lost per person[a]						
United Kingdom	0·012	5·500	0·759	0·127	0·309	0·693
United States	0·091	2·992	0·846	1·448	0·529	0·852
Comparative strike ratio (UK = 1·00)	7·58	0·54	1·11	11·40	1·71	1·23
Comparative productivity ratio (UK = 1·00)	1·94	6·91	2·68	1·55	2·55	2·51

Sources: OECD, *Labour Force Statistics*; UK, *Annual Abstract*; US, *Statistical Abstract*.
[a] Average number of days lost 1973–5, related to civilian employment 1974.

Strike incidence measured in this fashion is higher in the United States than in the United Kingdom for the industrial sector as a whole, and in all sectors other than the extractive industries.[3] It should be appreciated that the number of days lost through strikes is by no means a comprehensive indicator of the disruptive effect of poor industrial relations on output and productivity, and a superior British record in

[1] Were construction given the top labour quality ratio, the sectoral association between relative labour force quality and comparative productivity would be quite high for the Anglo-German comparison. Credence is given to the above analysis by the degree of inter-country stability in sectors ranked by average compensation per employee. Again, however, average compensation in the German construction industry seems out of line.

[2] On a comparable basis.

[3] Strike incidence in British extractive industries was inflated by the miners' strike of 1974.

this respect is by no means inconsistent with a significantly better American productivity performance. Whilst lower strike activity might be conducive to higher labour productivity, its effect could be swamped by factors working in the opposite direction.

Table 4.7 points towards an association between the sectoral patterns of comparative US/UK productivity and of comparative US/UK strike action. When ordered by the former ratios from the highest to the lowest, and by the latter ratios from the lowest to the highest, the sectors fall into an identical sequence: extractive industries, manufacturing, utilities and transport, agriculture and construction[1]

It is worthwhile emphasising the apparently high rate of days lost in American construction. A feature of our results is the unduly poor productivity performance of American construction and the especially good record of the corresponding German sector. The previous section drew attention to potentially advantageous characteristics of the German construction labour force; the apparent strike-proneness of the American construction labour force points in the opposite direction.

GROWTH AND PRODUCTIVITY IMPROVEMENTS

It is recognised that, at least within the manufacturing sector, a relationship exists between rates of growth of output and productivity improvements: by and large, those manufacturing industries experiencing above average growth rates also enjoy the higher rates of increase of labour productivity.[2] There has been rather less agreement about the causal sequences from which this relationship derives. On the one hand, it has been argued, above average productivity improvements may themselves generate high output growth via a reduction in unit costs and relative prices, leading to an extension of demand for the products of the industry in question. On the other, it is suggested, a rise in the demand for, and output of, a given industry's products fosters above average productivity increases via the realisation of economies of scale, the introduction of new capital equipment and the adoption of the latest production techniques. Conceivably both, mutually supportive, sequences may operate. In any event, it would seem that in some measure the manufacturing industry productivity differentials which obtain at any given time owe something to recent patterns of growth.

[1] Some confidence in the data on which this test is based can again be derived from a similarity between the two countries in the sectoral patterns of strike-proneness. In both countries, extractive industries lost most days per man, agriculture the fewest. The correlation coefficient between comparative strike action and comparative productivity is $-0{\cdot}56$.

[2] The original, 'Verdoorn's law', has over the years received considerable empirical support.

Table 4.8. *Sectoral output and productivity changes, 1968–77*

Indices, 1968 = 100

	Agriculture	Extractive industries	Manu-facturing	Con-struction	Public utilities	Transport
United Kingdom						
Output	120	124	110	85	140	128
Productivity	155	169	123	102	172	139
United States						
Output	116	115	123	97	137	141
Productivity	134	87	124	84	124	140
Germany						
Output	108	95	131	113	197[a]	141
Productivity	164	128	139	130	188[a]	138
Relatives UK = 1·00						
Relative US/UK change						
Output	0·97	0·93	1·12	1·14	0·98	1·10
Productivity	0·86	0·51	1·01	0·82	0·72	1·01
Relative Germany/UK change						
Output	0·90	0·77	1·19	1·33	1·47[a]	1·10
Productivity	1·06	0·76	1·13	1·27	1·16[a]	0·99

[a] 1968–76

It is relevant to enquire whether this relationship applies in any degree to all industrial activities – to the six sectors embraced by this study – and thus whether it helps to shape the international productivity ratios observed at the end of the period. It is appropriate to consider two possible relationships: whether, within each of the three countries taken separately, high growth sectors also display above average rates of improvement in productivity; and whether, for a given sector, inter-country differences in rates of growth of productivity are positively associated with international differentials in rates of growth of output.

Table 4.8 sets out the data required for these tests. It suggests that the first hypothesis is valid to a remarkable degree: that within each of the three countries sectoral output and productivity changes are quite highly correlated.[1] Only transport in the case of the United Kingdom and Germany, and agriculture in the case of the United States and Germany, are noticeably out of line: the former having a rather lower productivity improvement than expected on the basis of output changes, and the latter a better than anticipated productivity performance.

[1] The correlation coefficients for output and productivity changes over the six sectors are +0·89, +0·77 and +0·75 for the United Kingdom, and United States and Germany respectively. It is perhaps significant that productivity fell in American construction, that the lowest UK productivity rise was in construction, and that the lowest German productivity rise was in extractive industries – all sectors in which, in the country in question, output failed to rise.

There was also considerable common experience between the three countries in the sectoral patterns of output changes. The output of the public utilities and transport sectors increased relatively rapidly in each, whilst construction was a laggard in the United Kingdom and United States – with output actually declining – as were extractive industries in the United States and Germany. Associated with these influences are relatively high productivity rises in British utilities, extractive industries, and agriculture; productivity boosts in American communications, agriculture, utilities and manufacturing – with actual falls registered by extractive industries and construction; and the best German performance in utilities and agriculture.

Table 4.8 enables us to consider the second and, in the context of this study, more germane possibility: that for a given sector relative productivity changes between countries are positively associated with relative output changes. Thus, for instance, the table shows that over this period British agricultural output grew at 97 per cent of the United States rate, with British agricultural productivity rising at 86 per cent of America's.

There emerges a positive, if less than perfect, association between patterns of relative output and relative productivity growth in both pairs of country comparisons.[1] For instance the American manufacturing and transport sectors enjoyed both relatively rapid growth and productivity improvement compared with their British counterparts, whereas American agriculture, extractive industries and public utilities fared badly, on both counts, compared with corresponding British activities. German construction, public utilities and manufacturing were better than British counterpart activities in the case of both comparative output and productivity growth, German extractive industries were relatively worse on both scores.

Thus there is some evidence that over this period differential international growth rates, for each sector, by being associated with and to the extent that they induce differential productivity growth rates, have contributed to the current patterns of international productivity ratios. That this growth influence is far from being a complete explanation of these patterns is demonstrated by a comparison of the sectoral patterns of relative productivity *changes* in table 4.8 with the patterns of productivity ratios in table 1.1. There is a marked lack of any positive association between the way in which the British sectors' productivities have changed *vis-à-vis* those of the United States, and the sectoral productivity differentials which obtained in 1968 or 1977. In the case of the Germany/UK comparison, similarly, there is no positive association

[1] The correlation coefficient is +0·75 in the US/UK comparison and +0·83 in the Germany/UK comparison. A US/Germany comparison yields a much lower coefficient, +0·31.

Table 4.9. *Sectoral productivity changes in relation to sectoral output changes*[a]

	United Kingdom (1968–77)	United States (1968–77)	Germany (1968–76)
Agriculture	1·29	1·16	1·52
Extractive industries	1·36	0·76	1·35
Manufacturing	1·12	1·01	1·06
Construction	1·20	0·86	1·15
Public utilities	1·23	0·91	0·95
Transport	1·09	0·99	0·98

[a] Productivity index divided by output index

between relative productivity changes and the 1968 pattern of sectoral productivity ratios, though there is some suggestion that by 1977 recent relative changes in productivity were beginning to influence the Germany/UK pattern of productivity ratios.

There is one further aspect of international sectoral productivity changes which is of more than passing interest since it reflects well on Britain's performance. The improvement in British industrial productivity in this period was below that registered in Germany, better than that in the United States. However, when allowance is made for the effect identified above, the boost to productivity associated with output growth, Britain's improvement emerges in a more favourable light. This is demonstrated by table 4.9 in which for each sector and each country productivity changes are expressed as a ratio of output changes.[1]

It can be seen that in all British sectors productivity improved faster than output, a generalisation which can be applied neither to the US nor to Germany. Even more significantly, in only one case, that of German agriculture, was the productivity/output performance superior to Britain's. In sum, our productivity improvement tended to outstrip America's whether or not an allowance is made for different growth rates, and overall, would seem superior to Germany's when such an adjustment is made.

[1] The relatives which emerge from this procedure in table 4.9 are also the reciprocals of changes over the period in the various sectoral labour forces. This simply reflects the fact that labour requirements are determined by output and labour productivity levels.

5

PRODUCTIVITY DIFFERENCES AND SECTORAL CHARACTERISTICS

In the light of the results presented in chapter 4 our original expectations – that a search for factors exerting a common systematic effect on the productivity ratios of all six sectors would prove largely fruitless – were perhaps unduly pessimistic. Whilst the results are far from conclusive they suggest that one or two factors may well have such a general influence. In the case of other factors the evidence suggests that they may significantly influence productivity levels in certain sectors but not in others.

In this chapter we carry the quest for causal influences on productivity differentials a step further by focussing attention on special characteristics of the various sectors which might materially influence their comparative labour productivity performance. Included among these – where possible and relevant – is the manner in which productivity levels in component activities contribute to the sector's overall comparative labour productivity record.

AGRICULTURE

With certain reservations about labour inputs, productivity measurement in agriculture proved to be comparatively straightforward. Similarly, the international differences which emerge in agricultural productivity levels are somewhat less difficult to explain, at least in terms of proximate factors, than those in other sectors.[1]

Arithmetically, labour productivity in agriculture can be decomposed into two elements: yield per unit area and unit area per labour input. That is,

$$Y/L = A/L \times Y/A$$

where Y = output, L = labour input and A = area.

Studies of international differences in agricultural labour productivity are often based on this framework, a fairly recent one suggesting that,

[1] Because it proved impracticable to measure labour productivity ratios separately for forestry, fishing and agriculture, or for different kinds of agriculture, it is impossible to analyse productivity differences by sub-activity in the case of this sector.

Table 5.1. *Agricultural yields and labour intensities, 1970*

UK = 1·00

	Labour productivity ratio (*Y/L*)	Ratio of agricultural yield (*Y/A*)	Ratio of land per person (*A/L*)
US/UK	1·80	0·38	4·75
Germany/UK	0·75	2·07	0·36

Source: Yamada and Ruttan, 'International Comparisons of Productivity in Agriculture'.

in 1970, the comparative US/UK agricultural labour productivity ratio was 1·80 and the Germany/UK ratio 0·75.[1] These results compare with those in table 1.1 of 2·40 and 0·70 respectively. In part the discrepancies may be due to the probability that the weights used by Yamada and Ruttan for converting agricultural outputs to units of 'wheat equivalent' differ from the prices used in this study.[2] But some of the discrepancy is likely to be accounted for by differing treatments of labour inputs.

In any event the discrepancies are not such that the explanations put forward by Yamada and Ruttan cannot be applied to our findings. To be precise, they calculated that the agricultural productivity differentials arose in the manner shown in table 5.1.

In brief, agricultural yield (output per acre) in the United States is only a fraction of that in the United Kingdom, but the impact of this on the labour productivity differential is much more than outweighed by the 'extensive' nature of American farming: the amount of land used per unit of labour input is nearly five times the British level. In the Germany/UK comparison the opposite is found: in this case a higher German yield is more than outweighed by the fact that land per worker in the United Kingdom is about three times the German level.

As can be seen, capital – an important influence on labour productivity in this as in other sectors – plays no explicit role in this very simplistic model, and it should be reiterated that such an analysis assists only in the identification of immediate, proximate, determinants of labour productivity performances. Going beyond these proximate causes of differences in agricultural productivity, contrasts in the amount of labour applied per unit of land are largely reflected, and are dependent on variations betweeen countries, in agricultural capital (the number of tractors etc.) per worker. Similarly, differences in agricultural yields reflect not only labour cultivation intensities, but are also dependent on

[1] Saburo Yamada and Vernon W. Ruttan, 'International Comparisons of Productivity in Agriculture', in J. W. Kendrick and B. N. Vaccara (eds.), *New Developments in Productivity Measurement and Analysis*, NBER, Chicago and London, University of Chicago Press, 1980, pp. 509–594.

[2] It is not clear what weights Yamada and Ruttan in fact used.

the use of such non-labour inputs as fertilisers. Another major determinant of agricultural labour productivity levels, and contrasts therein, is farm size. It is recognised that German farms are generally smaller than British farms and that this contributes much to their high labour intensity, high yield and low labour productivity.[1]

EXTRACTIVE INDUSTRIES

The period with which we are concerned witnessed a dramatic improvement in Britain's comparative productivity in this sector *vis-à-vis* both the United States and Germany. The US/UK ratio was almost halved, from 6·68 – by far the highest sectoral ratio – in 1968, to 3·42 in 1977. The Germany/UK ratio fell from 2·00 in 1968, again the highest in that year, to 1·51 in 1977. No doubt more recent years have witnessed further narrowing of these differentials in Britain's favour. These developments are almost entirely due to the appearance of a single new, high productivity, economic activity: the extraction of oil and natural gas from the North Sea. Productivity developments in the other two sub-sectors, coal mining and other extractive activities,[2] contributed little to this dramatic improvement. Table 5.2 shows that in the case of the US/UK comparison, the coal mining ratio improved only slightly from 8·55 in 1968 to 7·60 in 1977, as did the 'other mining' ratio, from 2·08 to 1·82, whilst in the case of the Germany/UK comparison both ratios widened, in coal mining from 2·23 to 2·64 and in 'other mining' from 1·19 to 1·40.

Table 5.2. *Comparative productivity in the extractive industries, 1968 and 1977*

UK = 1·00

	1968		1977	
	US/UK	Germany/UK	US/UK	Germany/UK
Coal mining	8·55	2·23	7·60	2·64
Petroleum and natural gas			0·22	0·32
Other mining	2·08	1·19	1·82	1·40
Extractive industries	6·68	2·00	3·42	1·51

Source: Part II.

Clearly, changes in this sector's productivity differentials have been greatly influenced by structural developments. Indeed, more than in any other sector inter-country contrasts in extractive industry productivity

[1] D. K. Britton, *The Development of Agriculture in Germany and the UK: 4, A Comparison of Output, Structure and Productivity*, Centre for European Agricultural Studies, Wye College, 1981.

[2] The extraction of stone, slate, chalk, clay, sand and gravel, etc.

levels owe much to structural considerations. The situation fulfils both conditions necessary for a significant structural impact: absolute labour productivity levels which differ substantially between the sector's component activities and a sub-sectoral composition which varies greatly between the three countries.

In 1977, in the United Kingdom, absolute labour productivity (net output per man) in 'other mining' was more than twice the level in coal mining, and productivity in oil and gas some 15 times greater than in 'other mining'.[1] As for the sector's structure in 1977 coal mining still dominated in Britain with 86 per cent of employment, oil and gas in the United States with 49 per cent and 'other mining' bulked large in Germany with 49 per cent of employment.[2] In 1968 the structural contrasts were even starker than these. At that time the extraction of gas or oil in the United Kingdom was virtually non-existent, so that a productivity comparison between the United Kingdom and the United States was essentially one between coal mining, a low labour productivity activity, and oil and gas extraction, an especially high productivity activity. This contributed much to the very high US/UK ratio, 6·68, measured for 1968.

Inevitably therefore, structural considerations help to explain why, *vis-à-vis* the United States, our performance in this sector, despite recent dramatic improvements, remains especially poor. When the 'structural' and 'productivity effects' are separated in the manner described in chapter 3, it emerges that had the United Kingdom experienced, in 1977, the extractive industry output pattern which characterised the United States, productivity in the British industry would have been a third higher, and the comparative US/UK ratio 2·56 instead of 3·42. In sharp contrast, in the 1977 Germany/UK comparison, structural factors favour the United Kingdom as a result of our oil and gas production. With the German output pattern, productivity in the British industry would have been almost a quarter less and the comparative Germany/UK ratio 1·99 rather than 1·51.

It is plain that after allowance for structural effects there remain in both pairs of country comparisons significant differences in the productivity ratios to the overall detriment of the United Kingdom. Despite the boost to British productivity performance from oil and gas extraction – where table 5.2 reveals us in 1977 to be several times better than either the United States or Germany – the productivity level in the British extractive industry remains significantly inferior to that of the United

[1] The 1972 US *Census of Manufactures* indicates that productivity in gas and oil extraction was about twice the level in other extractive industries and about $2\frac{1}{2}$ times the level in coal mining.

[2] Partly as a result of differences in statistical coverage. See chapter 9.

States or Germany as a result of poor performances in 'other mining' and, especially, coal mining.

The same table points towards a considerable degree of stability in the sub-sectoral productivity ratios, both over time and in the country comparisons. On both pairs of country comparisons, the British performance is worst in coal mining, best (actually in absolute terms) in gas and oil extraction, and intermediate in 'other mining'. It is instructive that the implicit US/Germany ratios follow the US/UK pattern.

An important feature of the coal mining results in table 5.2 is the extent to which productivity in the United States exceeds not only British but also German levels. One explanation concerns opencast mining. The British coal mining results relate to deep mines only; opencast coal mining, which constitutes only a small proportion of total British coal production, is classified to construction. However, the data embrace opencast coal mining both in the United States, where in the late 'seventies more than half of coal production fell into this category, and in Germany, where the opencast contribution is also greater than in the United Kingdom. These structural contrasts assume significance because of pronounced differences in absolute productivity levels in the two kinds of coal extraction: in 1977, net output per head in British open cast coalmining was 90 per cent greater than in deep mining. In part, therefore, the poor British performance in this activity can be traced to this factor.

The early mechanisation of United States coal mining is another important consideration. The American industry is renowned for the extent to which it pioneered the search for large productivity boosts from mechanisation, and the degree to which it was welcomed – indeed fostered – by the mining unions.

In sharp contrast to our coal mining performance, *vis-à-vis* both the United States and Germany, is the current position in oil and gas extraction. The results would seem to show that British productivity in this sector is currently several times better than American and German productivity. A clue to a major explanation of these differentials lies in the US/Germany ratio which suggests higher productivity in Germany – where such extraction is on a small scale – than in the United States. The explanation resides in the fact that the labour forces of this sub-sector embrace low productivity exploration workers as well as operatives: in the early days of the development of British North Sea reserves the productivity of the workers involved would be effectively nil in terms of oil produced per man.[1] Once the products, especially oil,

[1] American data suggest that net output per operative engaged in the actual extraction of petroleum and gas may be six times the level of net output per worker in drilling and exploration.

came 'on stream' in the late 1970s, and the proportion of the labour force concerned with exploration declined, labour productivity soared.

Since the oil crisis of 1973, the United States industry has experienced the opposite sequence: a rapid rise in the number of workers engaged in exploration work, and a consequent decline in productivity. In short, much of the US/UK differential in oil and gas extraction is due to the fact that in 1977 the industries were at opposite stages of the development cycle: the British industry being 'on stream', the American much concerned with exploration. No doubt the development of a completely new industry, possessing the latest technology and with brand new equipment, also contributes much to Britain's superiority in this activity.

It should be noted that the Germany/UK comparison for 'other mining' is somewhat distorted by the unavoidable coverage, in the case of the German data, of much processing of the extracted stone, slate, chalk, clay, sand and gravel etc.[1] This difference contributes to the apparently disproportionately large size of this activity in Germany. In the present context the discrepancy is significant for its implications in terms of net output per man. The British census of production reveals that labour productivity in order XVI, 'bricks, pottery, glass and cement' – to which these processing activities are mainly classified in Germany – was no more than half the level in 'other mining', which suggests that German productivity in 'other mining' may, in consequence, be understated relative to British.

MANUFACTURING

In chapter 6 an attempt is made to identify the factors – size of markets, degree of integration etc. – which are responsible for differences in manufacturing productivity levels in the United Kingdom, United States and Germany. The findings are based on an econometric analysis of productivity ratios measured for manufacturing activities at the 'minimum list heading' level. At this juncture we seek to analyse productivity differentials in the manufacturing sector by identifying those activities at the 'order' level (or approximations thereto) which, respectively, boost or depress the relative performance of British manufacturing.

It is again instructive to consider the extent to which the sector's productivity differentials are attributable to structural considerations as opposed to productivity effects pure and simple. It can in fact be demonstrated that neither the US/UK nor the Germany/UK ratios are

[1] Processing which in the case of the United Kingdom (and United States) is classified as manufacturing.

Table 5.3. *The structure of manufacturing industry*

	Percentage of labour force		
	United Kingdom 1977	United States 1977	Germany 1976
Food	10·5	8·5	10·2
Petroleum products	0·5	0·9	0·5
Chemicals	5·6	4·7	7·2
Metals and mechanical engineering	26·3	24·0	27·8
Instrument engineering	2·1	3·2	2·1
Electrical engineering	9·6	9·6	13·2
Ships and vehicles	13·1	11·4	11·8
Textiles and clothing	12·9	15·0	9·4
Bricks, etc.	3·7	3·2	3·5
Timber and furniture	3·6	5·2	5·5
Paper	7·5	9·2	4·5
Other manufacturing	4·7	5·1	4·3
All manufacturing	100·0	100·0	100·0

Sources: UK, *Report on the Census of Production, 1977*; United States and Germany, estimates from Part II.

determined to any significant extent by 'structural' factors.[1] If the industry pattern of Britain's manufacturing output were the same as the United States',[2] then (with British productivity levels) our manufacturing labour force would need to be about ½ per cent larger. In the absence of this very slight British structural advantage, the US/UK comparative manufacturing productivity ratio would be 2·93 rather than 2·91. In the Germany/UK comparison it would appear to be Germany that enjoys a slight structural advantage. With Germany's output pattern our manufacturing labour force could be almost 2 per cent less, so that in the absence of this German advantage the comparative manufacturing productivity ratio would be 1·50 rather than 1·52.

However, it should be recognised that, theoretically, a small net structural effect could be due to a series of significant, but offsetting, contrasts in the structural make-up of the manufacturing sector in the three countries. That this is unlikely to be the case is demonstrated by table 5.3, which shows that taken all round the (labour force) structure

[1] For the distinction between the 'structural' and 'productivity' effects, and their separation, see chapter 3.

[2] It is more appropriate to apply this structural test than one based on the assumption that United States output is distributed on the British pattern since conceivably we could improve our overall productivity performance by changing the structure of British manufacturing industry. The two tests will not in general yield the same result – though the differences should not be great – because industry patterns of output per man are not identical in two countries.

Table 5.4. *Comparative productivity in principal manufacturing industries, 1968 and 1976*

UK = 1·00

	Comparative productivity ratios			
	US/UK		Germany/UK	
	1968	1976	1968	1976
Food	2·65	2·84	0·97	1·17
Petroleum products	2·54	2·06	1·53	1·54
Chemicals	3·05	3·28	1·55	1·62
Metals and mechanical engineering	2·43	2·60	1·39	1·63
Instrument engineering	3·57	3·16	1·14	0·95
Electrical engineering	2·71	2·56	1·00	1·03
Ships and vehicles	4·65	5·57	1·62	2·09
Textiles and clothing	2·23	2·26	1·24	1·45
Bricks, etc.	2·03	2·03	1·76	1·90
Timber and furniture	3·53	3·46	1·64	2·29
Paper	2·12	2·19	1·59	2·07
Other manufacturing	3·15	4·03	1·20	1·51

Source: Part II.

of manufacturing is quite similar in the three countries. This finding supports a conclusion of chapter 3, that it is not in structural factors that explanations of our poor industrial performance should be sought, but in productivity levels *per se*. Our poor overall manufacturing performance is due to the fact that in virtually every industry British labour productivity lies below the levels attained in either the United States or Germany. Table 5.4 reveals that in 1976 in only one out of 24 cases – instrument engineering compared with Germany – did we emerge as superior, and then only by a hair's breadth.

On the face of it, however, the results presented in table 5.4 would seem to suggest that our best and worst performances cannot be unambiguously identified: that it depends which country, the United States or Germany, we use as a benchmark. In the case of the US/UK comparison, bricks (with a ratio of 2·03), petroleum products (2·06), paper (2·19), and textiles (2·26), prevent the 1976 manufacturing ratio of 2·84 being higher than it is. In this comparison our worst performers are vehicles (5·57), other manufacturing (4·03), timber (3·46) and chemicals (3·28). In the Germany/UK comparison the industries which keep the manufacturing ratio down to 1·47 are instrument engineering (0·95), electrical engineering (1·03), food (1·17) and textiles (1·45). Our worst industries compared with Germany are timber (2·29), vehicles (2·09), paper (2·07) and bricks (1·90). It would seem therefore that we are comparatively good *vis-à-vis* both America and Germany in textiles; and especially bad in the manufacture of timber products and vehicles. To be set against this agreement is the observation that in paper products our performance is relatively good when matched with America's, bad compared with Germany's whilst the opposite applies to bricks.[1]

Whilst it is by no means impossible that these results reflect the actual state of affairs, there is evidence that the statistical errors inevitably involved in labour productivity measurement are clouding the true picture, especially in the case of the Germany/UK comparison. This is because differences in Anglo-German productivity levels are smaller in relation to margins of measurement error, than are the Anglo-American differences. On this score we have reason to place rather more faith in the observed pattern of US/UK differentials than in the Germany/UK pattern.

It is possible to test this explanation. If the foregoing argument is correct, then the (implied) pattern of US/Germany productivity differentials should also be more reliable than the Germany/UK pattern. Significantly this pattern accords quite well with that of the US/UK differentials. On both sets of ratios the three best European industries are paper, bricks and petroleum products, the two worst are vehicles and other manufacturing.[2] The agreement is by no means complete. Britain would seem to be considerably better than Germany *vis-à-vis* the United States in both instrument and electrical engineering, considerably worse in timber.[3]

Chapter 6 comprises a more detailed and sophisticated examination of the causes of international differences in manufacturing productivity. Unfortunately data limitations preclude, at the finer MLH level analysed in chapter 6, the application of a test which the contents of chapter 4 suggest might be revealing – for the possible existence of an association between comparative rates of growth of output and of productivity – a test that can be applied at the 'order' level.

Tables 5.5 and 5.6 indicate that the relationship within each country between growth rates and productivity improvements, noted in chapter 4 at the sector level, is repeated at the manufacturing industry level, especially in the United Kingdom and the United States.[4] Secondly, and

[1] A measure of the confusion in this picture is a correlation coefficient between the two sets of ratios in 1976 (US/UK and Germany/UK) of only +0·27. The coefficient between the two series in 1968 is +0·07.

[2] The correlation coefficient between the two series for 1976 is +0·60 and for 1968 +0·72.

[3] Though our reliability assessment suggests that measurement errors for this industry are perhaps the largest.

[4] The relevant correlation coefficients for these two countries in the period 1968–77 being, respectively, +0·86 and +0·70. The correlation coefficient for Germany over the years 1968–76 was much lower, +0·27.

Table 5.5. *Manufacturing industry output and productivity changes, US and UK, 1968–77*

	United Kingdom		United States		US/UK		Productivity change relative to output	
	Output index	Productivity index	Output index	Productivity index	Relative output change	Relative productivity change	UK	US
	(*1968 = 100*)		(*1968 = 100*)		(*UK = 1·00*)			
Food	115	123	131	138	1·14	1·12	1·07	1·05
Petroleum products	125	149	134	123	1·07	0·83	1·19	0·92
Chemicals	147	146	164	158	1·12	1·08	0·99	0·96
Metals and mechanical engineering	98	112	124	122	1·27	1·09	1·14	0·98
Instrument engineering	144	154	159	120	1·10	0·78	1·07	0·75
Electrical engineering	137	151	138	146	1·01	0·97	1·10	1·06
Ships and vehicles	95	102	110	120	1·16	1·18	1·07	1·09
Textiles and clothing	101	128	139	132	1·38	1·03	1·27	0·95
Bricks, etc.	106	130	138	131	1·30	1·01	1·23	0·95
Timber and furniture	103	117	130	118	1·26	1·01	1·14	0·91
Paper	108	122	125	119	1·16	0·98	1·13	0·95
Other manufacturing	128	124	179	155	1·40	1·25	0·97	0·87

more significantly, there is a positive association in both the US/UK and Germany/UK comparisons between comparative rates of industry growth and comparative rates of productivity improvement.[1] Thirdly the latter comparative rates of productivity improvement are in turn positively associated with the pattern of comparative productivity ratios which obtained at the end of the period.[2]

The changes depicted in tables 5.5 and 5.6 also afford some confirmation of a feature noted in chapter 4: that *in relation to the (relatively low) growth of output* experienced by British manufacturing, the improvement in our productivity has not been too discreditable. Compared with the United States, in eleven of the twelve industries British productivity increased more rapidly relative to output changes. Compared with Germany this is true of six industries.

[1] The respective correlation coefficients being +0·52 and +0·74. In the case of the US/Germany comparison the coefficient is lower, +0·27.

[2] The correlation coefficients for the US/UK and Germany /UK comparisons are +0·61 and +0·73. The coefficient between relative productivity changes and end period productivity differentials is equally high for the US/Germany comparison, +0·72.

Table 5.6. *Manufacturing industry output and productivity changes, Germany and UK, 1968–76*

	United Kingdom		Germany		Germany/UK		Productivity change relative to output	
	Output index	Productivity index	Output index	Productivity index	Relative output change	Relative productivity change	UK	Germany
	(1968 = 100)		*(1968 = 100)*		*(UK = 1·00)*			
Food	114	123	130	149	1·14	1·21	1·08	1·15
Petroleum products	115	133	114	134	0·99	1·01	1·16	1·18
Chemicals	142	143	159	149	1·12	1·04	1·01	0·94
Metals and mechanical engineering	99	115	123	138	1·24	1·20	1·16	1·12
Instrument engineering	141	151	116	126	0·82	0·83	1·07	1·09
Electrical engineering	129	144	166	147	1·29	1·02	1·12	0·89
Ships and vehicles	91	98	151	126	1·66	1·29	1·08	0·83
Textiles and clothing	101	132	108	154	1·07	1·17	1·31	1·43
Bricks, etc.	108	134	123	145	1·14	1·08	1·24	1·18
Timber and furniture	109	121	151	169	1·39	1·40	1·11	1·12
Paper	103	117	125	152	1·21	1·30	1·14	1·22
Other manufacturing	121	121	160	152	1·32	1·26	1·00	0·95

CONSTRUCTION

As explained in Part II, it was not generally feasible to measure comparative productivity for sub-sectors of this activity, a feature which hinders any structural analysis of the productivity differences that emerge. In the United Kingdom and United States absolute labour productivity (net output per head) is highest in civil engineering work, lowest in general building with the specialised trades also lying towards the lower end of this scale. When account is taken of these productivity differentials together with the distribution of the British and United States labour forces, neither country would appear to have a significant structural advantage.

However, there is apparently some bias in German construction activity towards the higher productivity civil engineering sector, which might help to explain the principal feature of our results for this sector: the pre-eminence of German construction. Other possible explanations of this phenomenon have been touched upon in chapter 4: the relatively large scale of German construction activity and special characteristics of its labour force.

The disproportionately large scale of German construction activities owes much to historical factors – even if of fairly recent origin. The post-war period witnessed an acute need for more housing, both to replace the stock lost during the war and to provide for the large influx of refugees from eastern Europe. On top of this the industry was obliged to supply the new industrial premises and plant required to sustain the especially high growth rate experienced by the German economy. It is little wonder that the sector came to be regarded as a bell-wether: that developments in construction are regarded, as appropriate, as forerunners of good or bad times for the German economy.

There is also evidence of the operation of a virtuous circle: success breeding success. Thanks no doubt to its high productivity and consequent competitiveness, the German industry was singularly successful in the 1970s in obtaining overseas contracts (especially in the Middle East). Certainly output levels have held up comparatively well in the face of the weakening of domestic demand that eventually accompanied the world recession.[1] The German construction industry has thus avoided many of the detrimental productivity impacts associated with under-utilisation of capacity which have afflicted both the United Kingdom and the United States.

A characteristic of the German labour force which has been cited as conducive to high productivity levels, is its foundation on hard-working immigrant labour. A further potential associated with this characteristic, and one amply demonstrated in recent years, is the ability of German construction to divest itself of surplus labour with comparative ease. Between 1973 and 1977 German construction output declined less than either British or American. Yet in the same period, when the British and American industries reduced their labour forces by less than a tenth, German construction shed more than a fifth of its workers. Not surprisingly these years witnessed cyclical declines of 10 per cent and 7 per cent respectively in British and United States construction productivity, but a continued improvement in Germany, by no less than 15 per cent.

PUBLIC UTILITIES

The comparatively high US/UK productivity ratio for this sector, 3·07 in 1977, reflects poor British performance in both the gas and electricity industries with ratios of 2·79 and 3·47 respectively. The ratio for 'water', the third and least significant activity of this sector, is quite low, 2·12. The same basic picture is found in the Germany/UK comparison.

[1] See chart 3·6.

Table 5.7. *Comparative productivity in public utilities*

UK = 1·00

	US/UK 1968	Germany/UK 1968	US/UK 1977	Germany/UK 1976
Gas	7·36	1·56	2·79	2·23
Electricity	4·06	1·93	3·47	2·25
Water	1·77	0·82	2·12	1·09
Public utilities	4·26	1·74	3·07	2·02

Source: Part II.

Again, overall, the UK performs particularly badly with high productivity ratios (in relation to the average Germany/UK performance) of 2·23 and 2·25 recorded in 1976 respectively for gas and electricity, and a ratio of 1·09 for water.

Whether or not structural contrasts in the make-up of this sector contribute much to the poor British performance is not easily determined. Certainly there are significant differences between countries in the relative importance of the various activities. In 1975 the gas industry accounted for 30 per cent of the sector's labour force in the United Kingdom, 23 per cent in the United States and no more than 14 per cent in Germany. The share of electricity in Germany was as much as 66 per cent, compared with 57 per cent in the United Kingdom and 53 per cent in the United States.

But such contrasts can play only a small part in explaining the comparative performance of the public utilities sector unless labour productivity varies significantly between the various component activities. If British census data were taken at face value, then net output per head in these three activities is remarkably similar – £14·3 thousand in gas, £15·1 thousand in electricity and £14·1 thousand in water[1] – in which case any significant structural contribution in favour of Britain or to its detriment is effectively ruled out. However, it is possible that pricing policies associated with the monopsony/monopoly position of the British gas industry – the sale of gas at increasingly higher prices relative to its cost – inflates the value of its net output and thus its apparent labour productivity performance.[2] Also, United States and German data (for 1975) point to significantly higher levels of productivity in electricity compared with gas, in the case of Germany the disparity being considerable. On this latter basis, labour productivity in British public utilities suffers from a structural disadvantage *vis-à-vis* both the United States and Germany because of the latter countries' compara-

[1] *Census of Production, 1977.*
[2] See Part II.

tively large electricity outputs. However, calculations based on American sub-sectoral productivity patterns suggest that the disadvantage is slight: 1 per cent in the case of the US/UK comparison and 3 per cent in the Germany/UK comparison.[1]

Again it should be recognised that more significant structural explanations might be discovered at finer levels of disaggregation. There may be substantial differences between the manpower requirements of coal-fired, oil-fired, hydro-electricity and nuclear power stations which, coupled with inter-country contrasts in the extent of reliance on these various forms of electricity generation, could give rise to a significant structural element in Britain's poor performance.[2]

Basically it would seem, however, that productivity differences, narrowly defined, are at the root of Britain's poor public utilities performance, in which case, in such a highly capitalised activity,[3] it would be logical to seek explanations on the equipment side. Perhaps British power stations are comparatively old – though it hardly seems likely that age of equipment would afford much of an explanation in the case of the rejuvenated British gas distribution industry.

A word should be added about changes in public utilities' comparative productivity. The principal development revealed by table 5.7 is the dramatic improvement in British gas productivity *vis-à-vis* the United States, a development which contributes to our overall improvement in this sector. It seems likely that this reflects the fact that at the beginning of the period the comparison lay essentially between British production and distribution of manufactured gas and American distribution of natural gas, whilst by the end of the period it was much more a comparison of like with like – simply the distribution of natural gas.[4]

TRANSPORT AND COMMUNICATIONS

The two conditions necessary for a significant structural contribution to international productivity differences are that absolute labour productivity levels vary between the relevant industries and so do the industrial structures in the countries in question. On both scores there would seem to be potential for structural explanations of the productivity differences

[1] These results are once more obtained on the assumption that British output is distributed, respectively, on the American and German patterns.

[2] The difficulty of obtaining labour productivity data by type of power station hinders a check for any such effect.

[3] In 1975, gross capital stock per man in the British gas industry was no less than £67 thousand, in electricity as high as £142 thousand.

[4] A sharp improvement implied in the performance of the German gas industry compared with the United States industry might be similarly explained.

Table 5.8. *Labour productivity and the structure of transport*

	UK Net output per head (£th)	Distribution of labour force (%)		
		UK	US	Germany
	1972	1972	1972	1970
Railways	2332	16	13	28
Road passenger	2300	15	8	9
Road haulage	2882	16	26	12
Shipping	4949	6	2	4
Ports	2817	6	3	2
Air transport	3851	5	8	2
Communications	3070	29	37	31
All transport[a]	2924	100	100	100

Source: See Part II.
[a] Including miscellaneous transport activities

which emerge from a comparison of the British, American and German transport and communications sectors.

Table 5.8 reveals that – at least in the early 1970s – the differences in British productivity levels in the sub-sectors of transport and communications were significant if not exceptional:[1] shipping and air transport display the highest labour productivity levels, and railways together with road passenger transport the lowest. In the case of this sector, however, the pattern of labour productivity levels in component activities is somewhat less stable than in others. The place occupied by railways, especially, differs between countries: in Germany, as in the United Kingdom, railways feature at the bottom of the transport productivity league; in the United States, for reasons to which we return, they are second from the top.

The other aberrant activity is communications. In Germany this is a low productivity activity, in the United Kingdom somewhere near the middle of the scale, and in the United States its performance in this sense is second to none. In part the position of communications varies so much because it combines, in different proportions between countries, two sub-activities, posts and telecommunications, that are characterised by contrasting productivity levels. British data suggest that output per head in telecommunications is about 75 per cent above the level in posts. When railways and communications are left out of account more similarity can be detected in international labour productivity patterns. In all three countries road passenger transport then emerges with the lowest output per head, shipping the highest.

Any attempt to determine whether patterns of transport productivity

[1] More recent comparisons are unavailable at the sub-sector level. For this reason changes in the patterns of comparative transport productivities cannot be considered.

align with patterns of capital intensity is complex even if attention is restricted to British data. For whilst investment embodied in the permanent way is included in railways' capital stock, road passenger and road haulage capital figures exclude roads, a form of capital which it would be difficult in any event to apportion between industrial and private usage. Nevertheless, it is clear that of the five sub-sectors identified above, the highest labour productivity sector, shipping, also enjoys the greatest capital intensity. It is also apparent that running the railways, with low productivity in the United Kingdom and Germany if not in the United States, is a highly capitalised activity. The presence of inter-industry productivity differentials does not by itself imply a significant structural contribution to international productivity differences: patterns of activity must also vary between countries. Such variations are revealed in table 5.8.

Given these conditions it is somewhat surprising to discover that the net contribution of structural factors to international differences in transport productivity is small. In 1972, labour productivity in the American transport and communications sector was 2·5 times the British level. Had the output composition of the United Kingdom sector been the same as the United States' then, with British sub-sectoral manning requirements, the productivity differential would have been 2·52 – suggesting a very slight structural advantage to the United Kingdom. In the case of the Germany/UK comparison, an actual 1970 differential of 1·21 is left virtually unchanged when allowance is made for structural factors. It would seem therefore that whilst significant individual structural productivity effects may arise in this sector, they are such that in the case of both pairs of country comparisons there is little net impact on the overall sectoral result.

Once again we are left with the conclusion that the sectoral productivity differences stem almost entirely from the contrasts in sub-sectoral productivity performance evident, in this case, in table 5.9.[1] Inspection of the table suggests there is no agreement between the patterns of US/UK and Germany/UK ratios.[2] Compared with the United States, we perform especially badly in railways, communications and ports, our best activity being road passenger transport. In sharp contrast, we actually do best, *vis-à-vis* Germany, in railways and communications (though still slightly worse in absolute terms), and least well in ports and sea transport. Such results would appear to highlight the ambiguity of

[1] Sub-sectoral ratios are available in the case of the Germany/UK comparison only for a single year, 1970; for the US/UK comparison, the principal results relate to 1972. Estimates for the United Kingdom and United States in 1968 and 1977 suggest that the subsectoral ratios for these various transport activities have been fairly stable, at least in terms of rank, over this period.

[2] The correlation coefficient is −0·45.

Table 5.9. *Comparative productivity in transport activities*

UK = 1·00

	US/UK 1972	Germany/UK 1970	Relative output scale US/UK 1972 (Rank)
Railways	3·95	1·08	2
Road passenger	1·34	1·34	6
Road haulage	1·80	1·27	4
Sea transport	1·70	1·90	7
Ports	2·48	1·95	5
Air transport	1·78	1·50	3
Communications	3·02	1·08	1
All transport	2·50	1·21	

Source: Part II.

the concepts of 'good' and 'bad' industries: it all seems to depend on the country of comparison.

Much more sense can be made of these results if the United States, rather than the United Kingdom, is made the fulcrum of the comparison. There is a very high degree of correlation between the US/UK pattern of transport productivity ratios and the implicit US/Germany pattern.[1] In both cases the United States excels, especially, in railways and communications, reserving its poorer performances for road passenger and sea transport.

Every attempt has been made in these sub-sectoral productivity comparisons to allow, where appropriate, for length of journey and the 'terminal work element' – the consideration that fixed transportation work elements (loading, unloading, etc.) bulk larger in relation to short journeys than long ones. This leaves a host of factors influencing labour productivity levels in the various transport activities which cannot be examined in detail in a study such as this: degree of capital utilisation, congestion factors, capital equipment, product mix, manning practices, etc. Nevertheless, it is possible to cite certain factors which may help explain why the United States is much superior to the United Kingdom (and Germany) in some transport and communications activities and only moderately so in others.

One possible explanation is that American transportation excels, especially, where its scale of activity is greatest relative to the United Kingdom. It emerges that the two sectors where United States market size[2] superiority is most pronounced are communications and railways,

[1] The coefficient being + 0·96. It was necessary to base this calculation on the 1972 US/UK pattern and a hybrid US/Germany pattern for 1970/72.

[2] Based on net outputs derived by the reverse valuation technique.

the activities in which US/UK productivity differences are largest, and the two where our own output most nearly matches American are road passenger and sea transportation where British comparative performance is best.

For statistical reasons it is difficult to test whether differences in capital intensity play a similar systematic role. But the available evidence suggests not. Both railways and sea transport are highly capital intensive sectors, yet in the former case the United States displays one of its best comparative productivity performances, in the latter one of its worst.

Again, one must resort to somewhat special explanations of the sub-sectoral productivity ratios set out in table 5.9. In the case of railways, a consideration which must surely contribute much to the pronounced superiority of the United States railways is the fact that, to all intents and purposes, they comprise a single purpose system. In 1972, 35 per cent of British rail traffic was freight, 65 per cent passenger; in 1970, the corresponding German railway percentages were similar, 31 and 69 per cent. By contrast freight was responsible for 97 per cent of American railway receipts in 1972, passengers for no more than 3 per cent. There must be enormous advantages in operating a freight-only system in contrast to the dual purpose railways of Britain and Germany. Added to this is the evidence that American railway labour force adjustments to technological change (especially to the abandonment of steam) were implemented more speedily and thoroughly, leaving fewer overmanning legacies, than in the United Kingdom.[1]

Differences in product mix may explain some of the marked American superiority in communications: the higher productivity telecommunications activity, rather than lower productivity postal services, bulks larger in America than in Britain. Moreover, redundancy problems in telecommunications associated with technological change were experienced at a rather earlier stage in the United States than the United Kingdom and the evidence suggests a smoother labour force adjustment.[2]

At the other end of the scale American productivity superiority is least marked in road passenger and sea transport and air transport too may be included in this group. A feature of these activities is that, in all three countries, they are carried out in broadly comparable conditions with similar capital equipment. Road passenger transport, including mass transit rail systems, is concentrated for the most part in urban areas so that the service faces basically comparable operating conditions – especially traffic congestion – in all three countries and uses similar

[1] See A. D. Smith, *Redundancy Practices in Four Industries*, Paris, OECD, 1966.
[2] Ibid.

equipment in the form of buses and underground rolling stock.[1] The same is true of sea transport: equipment, the kind of ships used, together with the transport medium, the seas, are essentially the same for all countries.[2] Air transport services too, in all three countries, have access to, and use, identical aircraft, operating for much of the time through the same airports. Of course other factors, such as management efficiency and manning practices, impinge on comparative productivity performances. Nevertheless, such a degree of uniformity in operating conditions imposes limitations which suggest that, in these activities, comparative international productivity differentials will be constrained within certain limits.

[1] In contrast lorries, their capacity and the nature of the roads on which they operate, may differ significantly between the three countries.

[2] Allowance having been made for productivity differences associated with coastal, open sea operations, etc.

6

AN ANALYSIS OF MANUFACTURING PRODUCTIVITY RATIOS

In this chapter we focus on the largest of our six sectors, manufacturing, attempting to identify factors which make some British industries more productive than others when compared with their American and German counterparts. Thus, the analysis pursues the quest initiated in chapters 4 and 5, but breaks new ground in two important respects: it is conducted at a finer level of disaggregation of manufacturing activity and, as a result, makes use of econometric techniques.

Specifically, we examine the 1967–8 US/UK and Germany/UK comparative labour productivity ratios measured and reported for manufacturing industries at, approximately, the level of the British 'minimum list heading' of the 1968 Standard Industrial Classification. Data limitations precluded an analysis for more recent years.[1] These productivity ratios relate to comparisons of net output per man standardised in British prices. Experimentation with comparative productivity ratios based on 'other country' price ratios pointed towards results not materially different from those presented here:[2] to avoid repetition they have not been included.

The overall distributions of comparative labour productivity ratios – relating to the manufacturing sector divided into 117 component industries in the US/UK comparison and 69 industries in the Germany/UK comparison[3] – are first examined. Next, certain hypotheses which are likely to be of relevance to explanations of differences in productivity ratios are considered on the basis of simple correlation analysis applied to the more reliable of these industry results. Finally, multiple regression analysis has been used to allow for the probability that international industrial productivity ratios are shaped by a number of factors operating simultaneously.

PRODUCTIVITY RATIOS FOR INDIVIDUAL MANUFACTURING INDUSTRIES

Productivity ratios for the 117 industries in the US/UK comparison vary widely, as shown in chart 6.1, from a value in excess of six to little more

[1] See chapter 10 where these comparative productivity ratios are set out.

[2] See also chapter 3 for a comparison of results based on British and 'other country' price weights.

[3] And providing complete coverage of the manufacturing sector in all three countries.

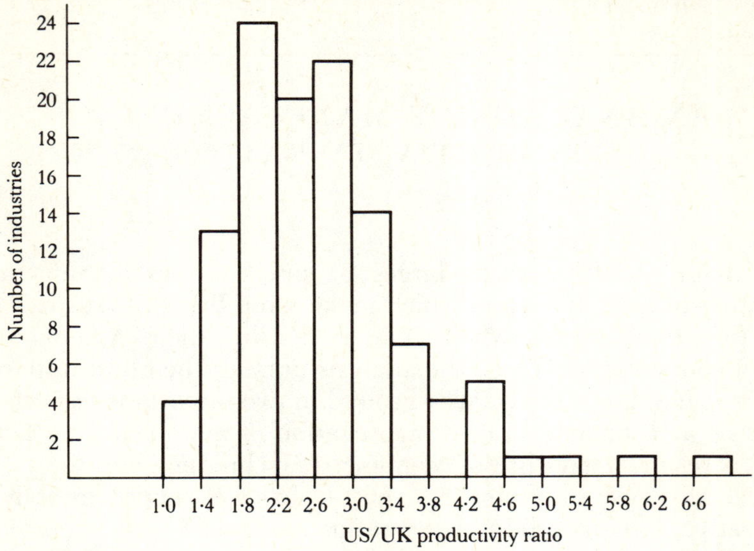

Chart 6.1. The distribution of US/UK manufacturing industry productivity ratios, 1967–8

than unity.[1] However, in almost 80 per cent of the industries the ratios lie in the range of 3·60 to 1·60, or approximately 33 per cent above and below the (unweighted) arithmetic mean, 2·69.[2] This distribution is remarkably similar to one compiled by Paige and Bombach for 119 US/UK manufacturing industry productivity indices in 1950, in terms of mean, range and positive skewness.[3] But probably the most significant feature of the distribution portrayed in chart 6.1 is that in not a single industry out of the 117 is British labour productivity higher than that in the United States.

The (unweighted) average of the Germany/UK manufacturing industry ratios depicted in chart 6.2 is 1·20[4] – otherwise the distribution is similar to that shown in chart 6.1. The ratios range from something in excess of three, down to a half, whilst the distribution is positively skewed with more than 80 per cent of readings within the limits plus and minus 33 per cent of the average ratio. In the case of this German comparison, it would seem that our labour productivity performance is inferior in about three quarters of the 69 industries.

[1] It should be emphasised that, at this stage, the ratios have not yet been screened for reliability.
[2] Compared with an overall (weighted) US/UK manufacturing ratio of 2·76 for 1967–8. See chapter 10.
[3] *A Comparison of National Output*, p. 63. The distribution in chart 6.1 is bunched more towards the mean than the one obtained by Paige and Bombach.
[4] Compared with an overall (weighted) 1967–8 ratio of 1·23. See chapter 10.

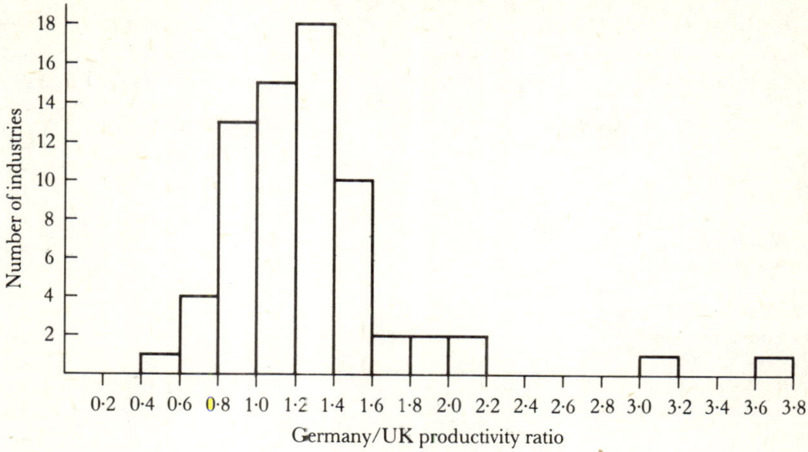

Chart 6.2. The distribution of Germany/UK manufacturing industry productivity ratios, 1967–8

By combining a number of the US/UK comparisons and some of the Germany/UK ones, it is possible to obtain on a reasonably comparable basis the three-way country comparisons of 62 manufacturing industries shown in table 6.1. If attention is restricted to our principal concern, a consideration of the US/UK and Germany/UK patterns of productivity ratios, it would seem on the basis of this table that identification of good and bad British performers depends very much on which country is taken as a standard of reference. In other words, there is little agreement between the patterns of US/UK and Germany/UK ratios: the correlation coefficient being less than +0·1. As in previous instances, however, a more systematic picture emerges if the United States rather than the United Kingdom is made the basis for comparison. The correlation coefficient between the US/UK and US/Germany ratios is +0·73, pointing towards the possibility of an underlying American/Western European pattern of ratios. As previously suggested the absence of greater agreement between the US/UK and Germany/UK patterns may reflect the possibility that in the latter comparisons measurement errors may be relatively large in relation to the size of the productivity ratios which emerge. If this is the case greater weight should perhaps be attached to the US/UK – and US/Germany – patterns.

The 'good' European performers appear to be cutlery, printing, pottery, agricultural machinery, 'other' building materials, bricks etc, milk products, miscellaneous stationers' goods and 'other' heavy machinery. The best American industries were vehicles, timber, aerospace, photographic and scientific equipment, biscuits, toys and games,

Table 6.1. *Manufacturing industry comparative productivity ratios 1967–8*

Industry	Comparative productivity ratios		
	US/UK	Germany/UK	US/Germany
Cutlery	1·14	0·79	1·44
Printing and publishing[a]	1·47	1·34	1·10
Pottery	1·49	1·11	1·34
Agricultural machinery	1·61	1·23	1·31
Other building materials	1·66	1·77	0·96
Sugar	1·67	0·49	3·41
Bricks, fireclay and refractories	1·69	2·09	0·81
Milk & milk products	1·75	1·21	1·45
Footwear	1·77	0·85	2·08
Misc. stationer's goods	1·79	1·50	1·19
Other heavy machinery	1·86	1·93	0·96
Ordnance	1·87	1·20	1·56
Shipbuilding	1·88	0·97	1·94
Cement	1·91	1·50	1·27
Spinning & doubling	2·05	1·36	1·51
Machine, engineers & hand tools[a,b]	2·08	1·30	1·60
Iron castings	2·09	1·10	1·90
Bread and flour	2·11	1·18	1·79
Woollen and worsted	2·11	1·18	1·79
Clothing[a]	2·12	1·02	2·08
Leather goods	2·13	1·34	1·59
Leather	2·15	1·00	2·13
Hosiery and knitted	2·19	0·92	2·38
Other mechanical engineering	2·23	1·37	1·63
Glass	2·29	1·41	1·62
Weaving	2·34	1·52	1·54
Meat & fish products	2·43	0·90	2·70
Textile finishing	2·43	1·29	1·88
Other wood & cork	2·43	1·45	1·68
Other metal goods[a,b]	2·46	1·29	1·91
Other food industries[a]	2·47	1·09	2·27
Oil refining, lubricating oils[a]	2·47	3·69	0·67
Bedding, furnishings (soft)	2·50	0·93	2·69
Other textiles[a,b]	2·54	1·37	1·85
Steel, coke ovens[a]	2·59	1·49	1·74
Electrical engineering[a]	2·66	0·94	2·83
Chemicals and man-made fibres[a]	2·75	1·38	1·99
Brewing and malting	2·77	1·04	2·66
Grain milling	2·78	0·66	4·21
Non-ferrous metals[a]	2·80	1·13	2·48
Rubber and asbestos[a]	2·80	0·98	2·86
Animal and poultry foods	2·82	1·47	1·92
Furniture and office fittings[a]	2·85	1·49	1·91
Fur	2·87	1·10	2·61
Fats[a]	2·95	1·82	1·62
Other machinery[a,b]	2·96	0·81	3·65
Printing machinery	2·99	1·47	2·03
Plastics and floor coverings[a]	2·99	1·32	2·66
Paper & board[a]	3·08	1·63	1·89
Cocoa & chocolate, confectionery	3·12	1·08	2·89
Office machinery	3·14	1·26	2·49

Table 6.1 (*cont.*)

Industry	Comparative productivity ratios		
	US/UK	Germany/UK	US/Germany
Surgical instruments and appliances	3·21	1·34	2·40
Toys and games	3·47	1·01	3·44
Biscuits	3·50	0·92	3·80
Watches and clocks	3·63	1·30	2·79
Tobacco	3·67	3·07	1·20
Photographic & scientific equipment	3·80	1·04	3·65
Aerospace	4·03	1·13	3·57
Timber	4·15	1·29	3·22
Misc. manufacturing	4·36	0·84	5·19
Other drinks	4·57	1·31	3·49
Motor vehicles, motorcycles & cycles[a]	4·58	0·99	4·63

Source: Chapter 10.

[a] Denotes a composite industry involving aggregation of 2 or more of those shown in the US/UK comparisons.

[b] Denotes a composite industry involving aggregation of 2 or more of those shown in the Germany/UK comparisons.

cocoa and confectionery, 'other drinks' and miscellaneous manufacturing. It should be appreciated, however, that at this stage the less reliable readings have not been omitted.

With manufacturing industry so finely divided, a test for the impact of structural factors on international productivity ratios is even more significant than those carried out in chapters 3 and 5. Again the test is based on the assumption that Britain's output pattern – in this case in the component manufacturing activities – were the same as that exhibited in, respectively, the United States and Germany. The results confirm that structural influences play only a very minor role in both country comparisons. In the US/UK comparison British manufacturing has a structural disadvantage of about 1 per cent – that is, the US/UK productivity ratio would be 1 per cent smaller had Britain the same manufacturing output pattern as America. And compared with Germany we enjoy a slight structural advantage – again of some one per cent.[1] Applying the same test to the individual manufacturing 'orders' reveals that in only a few industries do structural differences contribute much to the productivity differentials. In the US/UK comparison the effect is less than 10 per cent in all but three of the 17 manufacturing 'orders': Britain appeared to experience a structural disadvantage in

[1] The apparent unimportance of the structural factor is demonstrated by the small size of these effects and by the fact that the above results are contrary to those obtained for manufacturing in chapter 5.

Table 6.2. *Manufacturing industry sample coverage*[a]

Percentages

	US/UK sample	Germany/UK sample
Number of industries	50	48
Net output		
UK	44	59
US	44	
Germany		59
Employment		
UK	45	58
US	46	
Germany		61

[a] Percentage of complete results represented by the sample of the more reliable industry comparisons.

food and petroleum products, and an advantage in metal manufacture. As compared with Germany there was a structural disadvantage in petroleum products.

In the remainder of this chapter attention is directed to those Anglo-American and Anglo-German manufacturing comparisons considered to be the more reliable.[1] This has the effect of reducing our US/UK comparison to a sample of 58 industries and our Germany/UK comparison to 33 – about 50 per cent by number of the original comparisons. In practice, however, data limitations meant that the analysis was applied to rather fewer industries than this.[2]

As table 6.2 reveals, both samples are acceptably representative of their parent populations. The mean ratios in the samples do not differ greatly from the population averages, although in both pairs of comparisons they are slightly more favourable to the UK – in the US/UK comparison 2·61 and in the Germany/UK comparison 1·28. It would appear, however, from the output coverage percentages in table 6.2 that the US/UK sample tends to under-represent the larger industries, whilst the opposite is true of the Germany/UK sample. Nevertheless, both samples include a range of different sized industries and the results are unlikely to be affected by significant bias on this account.

PRELIMINARY CORRELATION ANALYSIS

In this section we begin to consider possible explanations of the picture which has emerged. For this purpose five factors have initially been

[1] Where the productivity ratios are accorded reliability indices of 1 or 2. See chapter 10.

[2] See table 6.3. Perhaps significantly two of the more extreme readings, involving UK industries with, apparently, especially poor performances, are eliminated in both pairs of comparisons.

Table 6.3. *Associations between explanatory factors and productivity ratios*[a]

Explanatory variable	Correlation coefficients			
	US/UK sample		Germany/UK sample	
	Comparative US/UK measure	Measure at UK level[b]	Comparative Germany/UK measure	Measure at UK level[b]
Scale as measured by:				
Industry net output	0·59***	0·02	0·53***	0·04
Industry employment	0·09	−0·12	0·13	0·0
Typical plant size	−0·27***	0·06	0·28*	−0·19
Capital intensity	0·18**	0·19*	0·02	0·22
Vertical integration	0·17	−0·22**	0·49***	0·06
Absolute productivity level	—	0·36***	—	−0·07
Degree of concentration	n.a	0·17	n.a.	−0·05

[a] Each variable has been correlated with the relevant pattern of comparative productivity ratios. Correlations for the US/UK sample are based on 45 observations and for the Germany/UK sample on 30 observations. In each comparison the sample comprises those industries for which the comparative productivity estimates are thought to be more reliable (see chapter 10) less a few for which capital intensity or plant size data were unobtainable. Definitions of the variables are provided in the text. Correlation coefficients which are significant on the basis of a 2 tailed test at the 20 per cent, 10 per cent or 5 per cent level are denoted, respectively, by *,** and ***.
[b] Correlations based on British inter-industry patterns of the relevant variables.

identified which, on the basis of the results of previous studies and/or the predictions of economic theory, may be of importance and for which data were reasonably accessible.

For most of the explanatory variables one can contemplate two ways of looking at the association with the patterns of productivity ratios. First, productivity ratios may be associated with inter-industry differentials in these factors, differentials which are implicitly assumed to be fairly stable between countries. Alternatively (or in addition) the productivity ratios may be associated with inter-industry differentials in the comparative international *ratios* of these factors. An example illustrates the difference. Assuming that the industrial pattern of capital intensity, i.e. capital per man, is similar in the United Kingdom, United States and Germany, it is relevant to ask whether Britain is comparatively good (or bad) in high (or low) capital intensity activities. But also it is pertinent to enquire whether British performance is comparatively good in those industries where capital intensity in this country is high relative to the United States or Germany – and vice versa.[1] British inter-industry patterns of the various independent variables – viewed in

[1] This latter test is not relevant in the case of labour productivity levels which, of course, would imply correlating the productivity ratios with themselves.

effect as surrogates of internationally valid patterns – have been used for correlations involving the first of these two kinds of test. The relevant correlation coefficients are set out in table 6.3.

The explanatory variables

Conventionally, the beneficial impacts on productivity levels of scale of activity are emphasised. Certainly economies of scale associated with longer production runs and the greater scope for specialisation which these afford should boost productivity levels. Moreoever, comparatively high productivity levels may in turn lead to a greater scale of operations via a consequent reduction in (relative) prices and an expansion of markets. On both scores a positive association between scale of operations and productivity levels might be anticipated. On the other hand this association might be blurred, or entirely offset, if larger scale operations induce a deterioration in labour relations and/or the impairment of management control as a consequence of long and fragile chains of command.

It has proved useful to distinguish between industry size – as measured by levels of net output and employment – and plant size. Industry size is perhaps the most appropriate concept for testing whether greater scale yields more scope for specialisation and higher productivity. In a comparatively large industry there should be greater scope for individual plants concentrating on single product lines yielding longer production runs. If the industry is small, however, firms may produce a range of product lines, impairing productivity.

Plant size is a rather more appropriate concept for examining those hypotheses concerned with economies of scale, management control and industrial relations: significant economies of scale might be achieved even in a small industry if there are only a few large plants. Scale of plant is measured by the midpoint plant size, in the sense that half the industry's employment is accounted for by plants in excess of, and below, that size.[1]

Another possible reason why labour productivity differs between industries and countries is the variation which can occur in capital intensity, the ratio of gross value of capital stock per member of the labour force. For the United Kingdom, capital stock estimates at this fine level of manufacturing industry have been obtained from official data relating to manufacturing 'order' levels disaggregated on the basis

[1] This is preferred to the typical plant size as measured, for instance, by the arithmetic mean, since it is a concept which is not unduly sensitive to the number of very small plants which can be encountered in the industry. (See S. J. Prais, *The Evolution of Giant Firms in Britain*, Cambridge University Press, 2nd impression 1981.)

of depreciation information taken from company accounts.[1] The American capital data derived from the census of manufactures are based on historical cost valuation.[2] German capital stock estimates[3] have been apportioned among our narrowly defined manufacturing industries on the basis of capital formation data taken from census of production sources. Undue reliability cannot be attached to the resulting estimates.

There is a widely held view that British industries tend to be less vertically integrated than their American counterparts. In some cases there are good reasons why this should be so: the British paper, tobacco and steel industries, for example, are all heavily dependent on imported raw materials and this clearly limits the scope for integrated production. Since there are often big savings (technological, transportation and administrative) to be derived from integration, differences between industries in the extent to which Britain falls short of overseas integration may exert an important influence on differences in comparative productivity.

To test this, the degree of vertical integration in a given industry has been measured by the ratio of value added to sales.[4] This is not an ideal proxy measure, but it is perhaps the best readily available one. Consider the car industry. Motor vehicle manufacturing includes not only car producers but also a large number of component suppliers. In those instances where components are 'bought in' by the car producers, their value appears in both the industry's total sales and purchases. Were these components produced only by integrated firms their value would not appear independently in either industry purchases or sales. In other words, with a greater degree of integration total industry sales are lower, whilst value added remains the same, so that the ratio of value added to sales is higher.

It is perfectly legitimate to examine the correlation between comparative productivity ratios and absolute productivity levels – net output per head. The test is applied to ascertain whether or not British performance is especially poor (or relatively good) in high (or low) technology industries as characterised by levels of labour productivity.[5]

[1] D. Elliott, 'Gross fixed capital stock in 1970 prices', National Economic Development Council, London, 1976 (unpublished). These estimates are consistent with the capital data used for the United Kingdom in chapter 4, and based on the perpetual inventory method.

[2] *Census of Manufactures* 1972, Industry Reports, Table 1.

[3] J. Frohn, R. Krengel, P. Kuhbier, K. H. Oppenländer and L. Uhlmann, *Der Technische Fortschritt in der Industrie*, Duncker & Humblot, Berlin, 1973.

[4] The data for this test were obtained from the relevant censuses when measuring productivity ratios. See chapter 10.

[5] Again the requisite data for this test were obtained as a by-product of the measurement of comparative productivity ratios. See chapter 10.

The long running debate in industrial economics about the advantages and disadvantages of monopoly, oligopoly and perfect competition suggests a variety of reasons why the level of seller concentration may affect labour productivity levels. Briefly one view is that industries characterised by high concentration achieve high productivity levels because the relatively few firms therein operate on a comparatively large scale and are therefore more efficient. The opposite view is that high concentration is associated with fewer competitive pressures and tolerance of inefficiency. In the case of this factor data limitations have precluded inter-country comparisons. It proved possible to test only for any association between labour productivity ratios and British ('five firm') concentration ratios.[1]

Interpretation of the correlations

Correlation coefficients between comparative US/UK productivity and the two measures of the size of British industry, + ·02 and − ·12, are in each case small and insignificant. Thus there is no evidence that the comparative performance of industries which are large in the United Kingdom is different from those which are small. This result does not imply that no gains are to be derived from operating on a large scale: a given industry may be large (or small) in both the United Kingdom and the United States so that any beneficial effect on British productivity of large scale operations could be cancelled out by a similar effect in America. It is of interest, therefore, to consider the correlation between comparative productivity ratios and comparative industry scale. Here, we find a positive correlation for both output (0·59) and employment (0·09) measures of industry scale, although only the former is significant, affording some evidence that productivity differentials are greatest in industries where the scale of British activities is small relative to their American counterparts. Although it can be misleading to attach unqualified causal interpretations to correlations, the results are consistent with the hypothesis that large industry scale is conducive to higher productivity levels, perhaps because of greater scope for specialisation.[2]

In the case of plant size similar results are obtained in the sense that there is little and insignificant correlation between typical British size

[1] Derived from the *UK Census of Production, 1968.* This concentration measure reflects the employment share of the five largest firms in the industry.

[2] It should be recognised that this analysis in effect involves correlating a (net) output figure with a productivity level in which the same output figure features as the numerator. To the extent that there are errors in the output measurement a spurious degree of positive correlation will in consequence arise. However, some comfort, and confidence in the validity of the above finding, might be derived from the presence of positive, if weak, correlation between the comparative productivity pattern and size as measured by employment.

and productivity ratios but an indication of a significant relationship between the comparative size of British and American plants and productivity ratios. In this case however the relationship is negative, pointing to larger productivity differentials (poorer British performance) in those industries where British plants are large relative to their American counterparts. In brief, the evidence is more consistent with the hypothesis that large plants are conducive to coordination problems and industrial unrest than that they yield economies of scale.

The capital intensity correlations are both positive and of some significance. They suggest that British performance tends to be poorest in the more capital intensive activities and also where British capital intensity is low relative to American. There is no conflict between these findings. Taken together they point towards a comparatively good British performance in activities where technology dictates only moderately capital intensive operations, with the British industry matching the American level of capital intensity.

The proxy measure for the degree of vertical integration, the ratio of value added to sales, is negatively correlated with the pattern of productivity ratios (with some significance) when measured at a British level, but in the comparative form is positively (and insignificantly) correlated with comparative productivity. Taken together, these results suggest a tendency towards better performance in the British industries characterised by a 'degree of integration' large both in absolute terms and relative to their American counterparts.

The two remaining variables are those which it was logical or practicable to measure at British levels only. Table 6.3 shows that there is no evidence of a strong correlation between comparative productivity ratios and British concentration ratios. However, a positive and significant correlation is revealed between comparative productivity ratios and British productivity levels. It would seem that British performance is especially bad compared with American in high productivity industries.

Relationships between productivity, capital intensity, plant size, concentration, etc. are best analysed on the basis of narrowly defined industries comprising sets of reasonably homogeneous firms. The German industrial classification especially does not permit this and therefore some of the manufacturing industries in our Germany/UK sample are defined at a level of aggregation which is inappropriately high given the nature of the hypotheses tested. Secondly, as pointed out in previous chapters, measurement errors in our productivity estimates are larger in relation to the Germany/UK differentials which emerge than to the US/UK ratios. Thirdly, estimation methods used for deriving German capital stock data were particularly crude. In the circumstances the relatively unsystematic and insignificant nature of the Germany/UK correlation coefficients shown in table 6.3 should perhaps not occasion undue surprise.

However, certain points of interest, and corroboration for some US/UK results, do emerge. In the case of scale of industry, the results tend to support the conclusion arrived at in the US/UK comparison: a suggestion that the larger the scale of British operations compared with German the better is the British productivity performance. Also, as in the US/UK case, there is a positive, significant, correlation between comparative productivity and the degree of comparative vertical integration: the more vertically integrated British industries appear to perform best.

On the other hand, there is a hint of a contrary conclusion to that obtained in the US/UK comparison about the effect of plant size. Using the comparative form of this variable there is weak statistical evidence (significant at the low 20 per cent level) that when British plants are relatively larger, higher comparative productivity levels are attained. An inspection of the data on this variable suggests a fairly simple reason for this apparent reversal of the US/UK result. In most of the sample industries, British plants are larger (in employment terms) than their German counterparts, but in the few instances where this is not the case (notably chemicals, metals and some engineering), German productivity performance is particularly good. It seems likely that the positive correlation recorded depends very heavily on these extreme observations – extreme, in that German plants are larger. Thus this result reflects not so much good British performance where plants are large relative to Germany, but more a British failure to achieve sufficiently large plants in certain industries in which German productivity is high and plant size is large.

REGRESSION ANALYSIS

A multiple regression analysis of the sample observations of comparative productivity enables us to consider the net effects of the above factors when they are taken as a group rather than, as in the previous section, separately and in turn.[1] Of the various formulations of an explanatory regression equation, the most revealing one in the case of the UK/US comparison is:

[1] Our present efforts have been confined to the productivity ratios and explanatory variables already introduced. Future work at the National Institute will embrace other variables and other countries.

$$[\widehat{CPROD}]_j = 1{\cdot}330 + \underset{(0{\cdot}047)}{0{\cdot}053}[CKAP]_j + \underset{(0{\cdot}028)}{0{\cdot}059}[KPLANT]_j + \underset{(0{\cdot}092)}{0{\cdot}195}[CVI]_j - \underset{(0{\cdot}079)}{0{\cdot}822}[PRICE]_j$$

$j = 1\ldots 45$, $R^2 = 0{\cdot}750$, $\bar{R}^2 = 0{\cdot}724$

where *CPROD* is comparative labour productivity, *CKAP* is comparative capital intensity, *CVI* is comparative vertical integration, *KPLANT* is typical plant size in the United Kingdom and *PRICE* is the US/UK price ratio.[1] All variables are measured in logarithms so that the coefficients can be interpreted as elasticities. Estimated standard errors are shown in brackets. The rationales for including all but the *PRICE* variable were considered in the previous section.

Leaving aside, for the time being, the *PRICE* variable, the interpretation of this equation is relatively straightforward: comparative US/UK productivity tends to be higher, that is British performance is especially poor, in industries which in the United Kingdom are less capital intensive than their American counterparts, less vertically integrated than their American counterparts and characterised by large plants. The latter two conclusions, though not the first, are fairly strong in a statistical sense, being significant at the 5 per cent level. However, in analyses which exclude the *KPLANT* variable, the *CKAP* variable also becomes significant at the 5 per cent level because of a substantially lower standard error. This is highly suggestive of the existence of multi-collinearity between the *KPLANT* and *CKAP* variables and, on this basis, we are reluctant to dismiss comparative capital intensity as a determinant of comparative productivity.

As stated, the formulation of the equation is such that the estimated coefficients can be interpreted as elasticities. So, for example, a 1 per cent reduction in the comparative US/UK capital intensity ratio (resulting from, say, a 1 per cent increase in British capital intensity) would 'lead to' a 0·05 per cent reduction in the British productivity shortfall. On this basis if we simply consider the size of the estimated coefficients, the variable *CVI* – comparative vertical integration – exerts the strongest influence. However the impact of these factors should also be viewed in the light of the degree of variability to which in practice they are likely to be subject. Certainly, in this sample, there is far greater variability in both capital intensity and plant size than in the measure of

[1] Variables are defined in the manner described in the previous section. The US/UK price ratios introduced are those (based on United States quantity weights) used to standardise each industry's net output as a prelude to the calculation of the comparative productivity ratio. See chapter 10.

vertical integration. Since the result relating to size of plant (*KPLANT*) is perhaps of special interest in a policy context, it is instructive to note that a 20 per cent reduction in the mean value plant size of 500 employees should yield, *ceteris paribus*, for the 'average' British industry, a labour productivity improvement of about 1 per cent.

The variable *PRICE*, representing the ratio of American to British prices, has been introduced essentially as a surrogate measure for comparative 'general efficiency', on the rationale that labour productivity differentials will be influenced by a whole spectrum of factors, other than those explicitly taken into account, which can be subsumed under the label 'general efficiency'. It is clear that such price ratios largely reflect comparative unit costs though other, non-efficiency, considerations such as differences in profit margins attributable to variations in degree of domestic and foreign competition will also be at play.

Certainly the results obtained for *PRICE* accord with the above rationale. In the US/UK comparison a significantly large coefficient emerges which is negative in sign: British industries which are comparatively 'generally efficient' (implying low British prices and thus higher values of *PRICE*) tend to be those where comparative labour productivity is high.[1]

In other experiments with the regression equation comparative capital intensity sometimes attains statistical significance at the 5 per cent level depending on the precise specification adopted. Also there is some evidence in certain formulations that the *level* of British capital intensity has a positive impact on comparative labour productivity, and

[1] There are two potential problems, however, when employing the *PRICE* variable in this way. First, there is the possibility of spurious correlation arising because these price ratios, which have been used to standardise international outputs for the productivity comparisons, are subject to error. The significance of this problem can be gauged by taking, as the dependent variable, productivity ratios based on a common price deflator, in practice United States output per man levels valued in $ related to United Kingdom output per man levels in £. This adjustment leaves undisturbed the results for the other variables and still yields a positive *PRICE* coefficient of 0·178 (standard error 0·079). Thus it is clear that the significance of this variable in the regression reported in the text is not merely the result of *CPROD* and *PRICE* showing a common measurement error.

A second problem concerns the possibility of a two way causal relationship between *PRICE* and *CPROD*, because prices are determined by labour productivity via unit costs. Ideally, therefore, the comparative productivity equation should constitute only one of a series of (at least two) simultaneous equations estimated by a more appropriate technique such as two stage least squares. In turn, this would necessitate a full theoretical specification of a price determination equation and considerable extra data requirements. Resource limitations prevented the pursual of this more ambitious model in the present project although it forms one of the objectives of the further work currently in progress at the NIESR. For present purposes, therefore, it must be acknowledged that the lack of statistical recognition of this two way causality raises the possibility of simultaneous bias in the equation reported in the text.

comparative plant size a negative impact, providing some confirmation of similar results in the earlier correlation analysis.

In the case of the Germany/UK comparison, the most revealing regression equation is similar to the one obtained for the US/UK but includes *CPLANT* rather than *KPLANT* (i.e. comparative, rather than absolute, plant size).

$$[\widehat{CPROD}]_j = 1{\cdot}09 + \underset{(0{\cdot}078)}{0{\cdot}118}[CKAP]_j + \underset{(0{\cdot}032)}{0{\cdot}056}[CPLANT]_j + \underset{(0{\cdot}229)}{0{\cdot}538}[CVI]_j - \underset{(0{\cdot}132)}{0{\cdot}505}[PRICE]_j$$

$R^2 = 0{\cdot}629$, $\bar{R}^2 = 0{\cdot}569$,
$j = 1 \ldots 30$,

The results relating to *CKAP*, *CVI* and *PRICE* are qualitatively identical to those recorded in the US/UK comparison. Comparative Germany/UK productivity tends to be higher, that is British performance especially poor, in industries which in the United Kingdom are particularly less capital intensive and integrated than their German counterparts and which record relatively higher prices (indicating generally lower efficiency). The latter two results (although not the first) are statistically significant at conventional levels. On the other hand, and confirming the earlier correlation results, the plant size effect is opposite to that found in the US/UK sample, though it is not significant at the 5 per cent level. In any event it is suspected that this result derives from the failure, in certain industries, of British plants to be operated at the (large) scale of German plants, rather than from a general tendency for British industries with larger plants to perform especially well.

The explanatory power of this equation far exceeds that which would be expected from the simple correlation analysis of the Germany/UK comparisons. However, it is based on quite a low number of observations (30) and the estimated coefficients are fairly unstable when alternative forms of the regressions are used. Bearing in mind our earlier reservations about the quality of the data in this comparison, there is, thus, less confidence in this result than in that reported for the US/UK sample.

7

CONCLUSIONS

This chapter summarises the salient findings of this study. It also appraises the study's conclusions about the nature of the factors which shape international productivity ratios and considers the implications of the results for British industrial policy.

THE PRINCIPAL FINDINGS

This study has attempted to measure, and go some way towards explaining, labour productivity differences in the industrial sectors of the British, American and German economies. For 1977 the results suggest that in terms of labour productivity American industry was some 2·7 times 'better' than British industry, and German industry some 1·4 times 'better'. It should be stressed that labour productivity is but one criterion of industrial performance and not the final arbiter of overall efficiency. Nevertheless, it is perhaps the most important single indicator of economic achievement. At the level of the economy as a whole, output per head is the basic determinant of living standards whilst in individual economic activities differences in labour productivity attainments have a major impact on international competitiveness. It is (and has been for some years) a matter of great concern therefore that British labour productivity should lag so far behind that of the United States and Germany – and of many other developed countries. Indeed, the unsatisfactory British performance constitutes the main *raison d'être* of this study.

The term 'industrial sector' has been interpreted in a wider sense than is conventional. It has been taken to include agriculture, extractive industries, manufacturing, construction, public utilities and transport, so that a more apt – though more clumsy – description of the study's coverage would be the non-service economy. This coverage represents 63 per cent of total British output, 52 per cent of American and 68 per cent of German. If some very approximate assumptions are made about comparative international productivity in the remainder of the economy, that is in service activities, it appears that for the economy as a whole the US/UK labour productivity differential is of the order of 2·0 and the Germany/UK differential is a little less than 1·4.

These industrial productivity ratios are relatively insensitive to alternative measurement techniques. For convenience, those quoted above, 2·7 and 1·4, are based on calculations using British price weights. If 'other country' (American or German) weights are used, British productivity emerges about a tenth better – a significant effect but one which does comparatively little to close the productivity gaps. On the other hand an allowance for international differences in hours worked – the principal comparisons in this study are of output per man year – suggests a widening of the productivity differentials to Britain's further disfavour by no more than about 10 per cent.

A principal feature of this study is that the comparative productivity ratios obtained for the industrial sector have been built up from productivity measures for each of the six component sectors. In this respect the work seeks to avoid undue preoccupation with manufacturing productivity to the neglect of our performance in other activities. Our approach enables us to consider explanations of Britain's poor performance from a viewpoint which has for some years been overlooked: an identification of those activities wherein, in relation to achievements in other countries, the strengths and weaknesses of the British economy are revealed. Actual responsibility for any shortfall in Britain's international performance is more difficult to allocate between sectors since the productivity performance of one sector is in part, at least, dependent on the achievements of others.

Compared with both the United States and Germany, British performance in the extractive industries and public utilities was for most of the 1970s especially poor, whilst a better record was achieved by agriculture and transport. In both country comparisons the British manufacturing sector's performance was near the industrial average whilst our construction industry fared comparatively well compared with American construction and especially badly compared with the German industry. It should be stressed, however, that in only one instance – British agriculture compared with its German counterpart – is British labour productivity superior in an absolute sense.

How much these individual sectoral achievements (or lack of them) directly contribute to the general British performance depends not only on the productivity disparity displayed for each sector but also on the size and importance of each activity in the industrial sector. When account is taken of the latter as well as the former consideration, not surprisingly perhaps it emerges that manufacturing accounts for more than half the industrial productivity disparity in both pairs of country comparisons. Also the construction sector accounts for much of the remaining difference in the Anglo-German industrial differential, and transport for much of the remaining Anglo-American difference. In the total industrial picture the other sectoral impacts tend to be comparatively small so that we reap little overall benefit from the superiority of our agriculture to Germany's.

The measurement errors inevitably involved in the estimation of these productivity achievements are unlikely to cloud the basic sectoral pictures which emerge, especially in the case of the US/UK comparison.[1] The reliability of estimation procedures is perhaps more questionable in the case of the productivity measures for certain of the sub-sector activities from which the sectoral results are obtained.[2] Even in these cases however it seems clear that compared with both the United States and Germany, British labour productivity is especially low, for instance, in coal mining, vehicle production and the generation of electricity. On the other hand a beacon of light shines in the revelation that in the extraction (from the North Sea) of oil and gas, we enjoy, by some margin, higher labour productivity.

In certain activities (for instance those in the transport sector) we emerge as comparatively good (or bad) compared with the United States but not with Germany – or vice versa. It is of course quite feasible that such results reflect a real state of affairs: that in many cases it is misleading to designate an activity as 'good' or 'bad' since it depends on the country of comparison. It is possible, however, particularly at the sub-sectoral level, that measurement errors especially in the Germany/UK comparison are confusing the picture – in which case rather more interest centres on the Anglo/American results. Some confirmation of this is provided by the pattern of the US/Germany productivity differentials which are implicit in our results. In many cases these patterns tend to align with those obtained for the US/UK comparison, hinting at an underlying American/Western European pattern of sectoral productivity differentials.

In terms of sectoral rankings there would seem to be no dramatic developments in comparative sectoral productivity patterns between 1968 and 1977. In the US/UK comparison there was no change in the sectoral rankings; in the Germany/UK case British comparative performance in construction moved down the scale (worsened) and in extractive industries moved up. Longer-term comparisons which are possible with the United States suggest that as far back as the 1930s the principal British laggard was extractive industry, and comparatively our best performers have been, for some decades, construction and agriculture.

[1] We feel measurement errors are rather more serious in the Germany/UK comparison especially in relation to the lower ratios which emerge.

[2] Productivity comparisons could not be made for component activities in the agriculture and construction sectors.

This apparent stability in sectoral rankings disguises some very significant changes in sectoral and industrial comparative productivity. In particular it is clear that, compared with Britain, the American economy benefited substantially from conditions during the Second World War and the immediate postwar period. The comparative US/UK ratio widened from 1·81 in the late 1930s to about 3·00 by 1950 – since when it narrowed to 2·66 in 1977. Between 1968 and 1977 in all six major sectors British productivity improved relative to American or remained virtually unchanged, yet the overall industrial ratio registered only a minor improvement, from 2·78 to 2·66. Part of the explanation of this disappointment is that the more significant improvements in comparative British productivity have been registered in the smaller sectors: a dramatic rise in productivity in British extractive industries thanks to the development of North Sea oil and gas; and a significant improvement in the performance of public utilities due to the transformation of the British gas industry from production to distribution. Thus our two worst sectors *vis-à-vis* the United States have also registered the sharpest improvements in comparative productivity, thereby substantially narrowing the range of sectoral productivity ratios. Much of the explanation of the disappointingly small overall improvement in our industrial productivity compared with the US resides in the fact that there has been little change in comparative British productivity in the largest sector – manufacturing. Clearly the environmental and technological windfalls which have come Britain's way in the last decade or so have been insufficient to make up the productivity leeway which, compared with the United States, we lost during the Second World War.

Between 1968 and 1977 the gap between British and German industrial performance widened. In this case a substantial improvement in comparative British productivity in the extractive industries did not offset deteriorations in public utilities, construction and manufacturing. Given the latter sector's quantitative importance, its performance has been particularly instrumental in the failure of Britain's industrial productivity growth to match that of Germany.

INFLUENCES ON PRODUCTIVITY DIFFERENTIALS

It is important for the future of industrial policy prescription in this country to obtain an understanding of the forces which have shaped the industrial productivity differentials measured in this study. It is plain that a complete identification of these forces – be they general or specific, physical, historical, institutional or economic – cannot be pursued, in detail, in a study concerned with all non-service activities.

Nevertheless, the results have been analysed in such a way that they yield indicators to the more immediate considerations which influence productivity levels and help to answer some of the more basic questions which have been posed in this context over the years.

One question which has aroused much interest is whether Britain's poor industrial productivity can be traced to structural imbalances in the economy: to the fact that our efforts and resources are concentrated in activities which in some techno-economic sense are 'wrong'. On the evidence which we have assembled the answer would seem to be no. At least, that is, there is no evidence that Britain's poor industrial productivity is to any significant extent due to the fact that compared with the United States and Germany our resources are concentrated in those industries where absolute levels of labour productivity (output per man) are low. In the main this conclusion holds whether we compare, between countries, output distribution among the six principal sectors, the sub-activities within a sector or among manufacturing industries finely specified. This conclusion emerges despite the fact that there are very substantial differences between sectors and industries in absolute productivity levels. Thus in essence it reflects the fact that, with one or two qualifications, the industrial structures of the British, American and German economies are not so very different.

The principal exception to this generalisation concerns extractive industries. A feature of this sector is the extent to which labour productivity levels differ between, on the one hand, coal mining and, on the other, oil and gas extraction. At the same time oil and gas extraction accounts for much of the sector's output in the United States, very little in Germany, with the United Kingdom occupying an intermediate position. As a result, America has a significant structural productivity advantage compared with Britain, and Britain a substantial advantage compared with Germany. Perhaps the importance of this factor is best brought home when it is realised that the very large US/UK productivity ratio registered in 1968 for extractive industries (6·68) reflected, essentially, a comparison between low productivity British coal mining and high productivity American oil and gas extraction.

If, generally, such structural considerations have little influence on the comparative British productivity performance it follows that our shortcomings are due to productivity effects pure and simple: that, industry for industry, labour productivity levels in this country are in most cases below those registered in the United States and Germany. It is logical and instructive to ask, in turn, to what extent these deficiencies are attributable to contrasts in natural resource endowments and thus apparently immutable considerations, and to what extent they might be attributable to technical and economic factors which in principal are amenable to policy prescription as a means of improving British performance.

There is no doubt that environmental factors (interpreted broadly to include historical influences) do much to determine the international productivity differentials which have emerged for certain activities. The poor productivity performance of the British coal industry, compared with either the United States of Germany, is in substantial measure due to the inclusion in the American and German industry of much opencast mining. The fact that British railway productivity is low compared with America's is in part due to the fact that American railways are effectively a single purpose system being almost wholly concerned with freight. This in turn can be ascribed to the competitive edge which longer American distances confer on air passenger travel. And it may be that the good German construction performance owes much to an historical accident: the enormous levels of demand with which wartime depredations and postwar conditions confronted the industry.

Yet, the first point to notice about this kind of factor is that by no means do they all work to Britain's disadvantage. Longstanding historical and social considerations are at the root of the small size of German agricultural holdings, the high ratio of labour to land which ensues and the low level of German agricultural labour productivity compared with British. Similarly, given Britain's oil and gas endowments compared with those of Germany our superiority in their extraction is hardly to be wondered at.

Secondly, it would be wrong to regard such 'natural' conditions as entirely immutable and essentially unresponsive to economic policy. The rate of exploitation of North Sea energy resources was to some extent, at least, a function of government policy as, no doubt, is the current balance between surface and deep-mined coal in this country and a rise in average farm size in Germany could probably be brought about by appropriate social and economic measures.

If Britain's poor productivity performance cannot be mainly explained in terms of 'environmental' considerations, to what other factors must we direct attention? Economic theory, and empirical research, have served to identify certain factors which probably do much to determine international labour productivity differentials. Part of this study has been devoted to an examination of possible relationships between the measured differentials and various such influences – scale of activity, plant size, vertical integration, degree of concentration, absolute productivity levels, capital intensity, labour force quality, strike action and growth rates. In the case of some of these potential explanatory factors it proved feasible to test for an association with international productivity differentials only at the major sector level. In others it was possible to analyse the relationships only within the context of manufacturing finely divided. For a few the analysis could be conducted at more than one level. Inevitably many of the tests of association – especially (in view of the very limited number of observations) those applied to the major sectors – were rough and ready, even impressionistic, in nature, though rather more sophisticated techniques were applied to the larger number of manufacturing industries.

We have been encouraged in this analysis by the fact that, despite the statistical imperfections to which the data are subject, fairly systematic patterns of results emerged. Moreover, there is little perversity in the findings in the sense that the occasions are rare where a relationship emerges between a causal factor and productivity differentials that contradicts theoretical or commonsense expectations. Below we distil from the analysis the more frequent and strong associations to which the results point.

First most tests suggest a positive association between comparative capital intensity (capital per man) and comparative productivity ratios. That is British performance tends to be inferior to America's or Germany's where the activity in question is under-capitalised compared with its overseas counterpart. This finding, taken in conjunction with the fact that in nine of the twelve inter-country sectoral comparisons the British activity appears to be comparatively under-capitalised, indicates that this weakness is responsible for some of our shortfall in productivity.[1]

Certain tests, especially those applied to manufacturing, suggest that patterns of comparative productivity ratios are associated with the industry pattern of capital intensity. That is, Britain tends to perform worst in activities characterised by high capital per man requirements. This finding is closely associated with another. There is evidence, especially in the case of the US/UK comparisons, of an association between comparative productivity ratios and absolute levels of labour productivity such that the higher the latter the worse is British performance. Britain has especially failed to attain high labour productivity levels in those activities where the productivity potential is greatest partly, but only partly, as a result of under-capitalisation.

Another influence which was considered at the level of both manufacturing industry and major sector is scale of activity. Elements in the analysis of manufacturing industries point towards the productivity differential being larger – Britain's performance being poorer – in industries where our scale of operation is below that in counterpart

[1] A thorough appraisal of the part played by capital in shaping international labour productivity ratios would require a parallel consideration of its own productivity, i.e. of output per unit of capital.

American and German activities. This suggests that in manufacturing large markets afford some opportunities for specialisation. At the sector level this association is not contradicted, but receives only slight support.

Tests for possible associations between size of establishment and international productivity performance pose problems both of principle and interpretation. In the case of transportation and construction the very concept of establishment is nebulous. In other activities, however, it is meaningful and highly relevant to test for such an association: there is little doubt that the comparatively small size of German farms limits their productivity performance compared with Britain's agriculture. But it is in the context of the manufacturing sector that possible relationships between plant size and performance are probably of greatest significance and are usually pursued. Our tests suggest that in the case of the US/UK comparison comparative British productivity tends to be especially poor in industries where plant size is typically large.[1]

It is also pertinent to enquire whether international productivity performance in the manufacturing sector is in any measure associated with the degree of vertical integration. In both pairs of country comparisons the results suggest that the more vertically integrated a British industry compared with its competitors the better is its labour productivity performance.

Some tests of association were implemented only at the level of the principal sectors. Since this implies a maximum of six 'readings' in each case only somewhat speculative inferences can be drawn from the results. In fact, given the degree of diversity in operating conditions between the sectors studied – between for instance agriculture and construction – it is remarkable that certain systematic associations are discernible. The results are not inconsistent with, and lend some support to, the possibility that both labour force quality and industrial relations exert an influence on international performance: that a tendency can perhaps be discerned for Britain to perform comparatively well in activities where, compared with other countries, our labour force quality is good and strike action low.

Analysis of productivity changes in the six major sectors and the twelve principal manufacturing industries reveals the existence of a relationship between comparative productivity achievements and comparative growth performance. More precisely, the analysis suggests three conclusions. First, in each country, there is a tendency for the sectors and industries enjoying the fastest rates of output growth to

[1] Evidence about any such relationship in the Germany/UK comparison is statistically weak and the analysis complicated by special features of the comparison.

record the largest improvements in labour productivity. Secondly, comparative changes in Britain's productivity are associated with our comparative growth performance; British productivity levels tend to rise most relative to American and German in those sectors and industries where our output growth rates have been comparatively good. Thirdly, in relation to the sectoral and industry growth rates actually achieved in the three countries, British productivity improvements have tended, if anything, to be better than those in the United States and Germany.

THE FINDINGS AND INDUSTRIAL POLICY

The main thrust of this study has been to identify the extent to which Britain's comparatively poor industrial productivity performance is reflected in the achievements of the principal sectors of the economy. For this purpose it has been largely preoccupied with the measurement, and international comparison, of sectoral labour productivity levels. To the extent that, additionally, it was possible to consider proximate and immediate causes of the international differentials which emerge, it is hoped that it will also prove useful as a launching pad for more detailed scrutiny and explanation of international sectoral productivity differentials. Only studies such as the latter can provide a sound basis for the formulation of an industrial policy which, *inter alia*, would be directed at redressing the balance between our own performance and that of other countries.

Nevertheless some pointers relevant to the basis of our industrial strategy emerge from the present study. First – and perhaps foremost – there should be no room, when considering Britain's industrial productivity performance and ways of improving it, for counsels of despair. Patently there has been an undercurrent of economic fatalism in the way our record has been regarded: a feeling that in some fundamental way the chips have been stacked against Britain for several decades and that little is to be expected from measures designed to reverse our poor performance. For the evidence suggests that, at least compared with the United States and Germany, we are not overburdened with low productivity industries. Differences in natural resource endowments explain only part of the observed international productivity differentials, by no means all operate to Britain's disadvantage and, in any case, are to some extent amenable to policy prescription.

Secondly, the results provide no comfort for those who would pinpoint a single overriding factor as the root cause of Britain's problem – be it underinvestment or low growth or poor labour force quality or, one may hazard, overmanning or inefficient management. For it would appear that a variety of factors determine, to a differential extent by sector, labour productivity ratios and Britain's poor industrial record. Consequently an essentially pragmatic, non-doctrinaire, approach for raising our performance has the greatest chance of success. An industrial policy to improve our record should not be geared to any single factor – say new investment or raising labour force quality – to the neglect of others. Moreover it is likely to be necessary to tailor-make policies, for individual sectors and industries, which promote a blend of industrial measures appropriate to the economic and technical conditions in question. For the present study has demonstrated beyond doubt that when judged by international yardsticks Britain's productivity performance varies very significantly from sector to sector.

Part II

THE MEASUREMENT OF PRODUCTIVITY DIFFERENTIALS

8

AGRICULTURE, FORESTRY AND FISHING

STRUCTURE AND METHOD

In each of the three countries, agriculture dominates this sector, acounting, in 1974, for 93 per cent of output in the UK, 91 per cent in the US and 84 per cent in Germany (see table 8.1). Within agriculture,

Table 8.1. *Structure of the agriculture, forestry and fishing sectors, 1974*

	UK (£m)	US($m)	Germany (DMm)
Gross value added at factor cost in agriculture, forestry and fishing	2067	49117	25857
of which: agriculture	1931	44917	21567
forestry and fishing	136	4200	4290
Employment in agriculture, forestry and fishing (thousands)	683	3588	1882

Sources: ILO, *Yearbook of Labour Statistics;* United Nations, *Yearbook of National Accounts Statistics*; see also text.

however, there are clearly some significant inter-country differences in the composition of output. It is fortuitous that agriculture bulks so large in this sector's activities since neither output nor labour force data are such as to promote productivity results of any reasonable reliability for forestry and fishing. On the other hand, in all three countries we are quite well served with output data for agriculture, though labour force concepts and measures pose problems.

For most agricultural products in the three countries gross output is completely specified in the relevant sources, physical, value and unit price data all being available.[1] It is therefore a relatively straightforward procedure to apply the basic methodology described in chapter 2,

[1] For the United States, the Department of Agriculture annual publication *Agricultural Statistics* satisfies the total data requirements. For West Germany and the United Kingdom, instead of using primary national sources, most of our calculations are based on data reported in the United Kingdom Ministry of Agriculture, Forestry and Fishing (MAFF), *EEC Agricultural and Food Statistics 1972–75*, 1976. This source (itself based on publications of the Statistical Office of the European Communities) presents data for the United Kingdom and West Germany (as well as other European countries) on a standardised and comparable basis. The United Kingdom (MAFF) national source *Agricultural Statistics* has also occasionally been used.

whereby in each country, physical units of various types of agricultural output are aggregated using both British price relatives and those of the 'other' country. By this means total agricultural output in each of the three countries (which cannot of course be allocated to particular sub-divisions of the agricultural labour force) may be expressed – 'standardised' – in the currencies of the other countries. The data also yield price ratios for each category of output and, suitably weighted, price ratios for total agricultural output.

There are a few production categories where output is not fully specified in terms of comprehensive quantities and unit values. In such cases the output values of the category in question are deflated to a 'standardised' output figure using a price index based on available selected products.

Participation of large numbers of self-employed, paid and unpaid family workers in agriculture renders estimation of the size of the sector's labour force in all three countries subject to considerable error. As a result, the productivity comparisons, especially those between Germany and the UK, prove to be especially sensitive to assumptions about the size of the labour force. Problems with labour force statistics are mainly responsible also for the lack of separate productivity calculations for forestry and fishing activities. To fill this gap the results obtained for agriculture have, in effect, been extended to cover the whole sector, though since agriculture plays such a dominant role in the sector this should not unduly impair the overall conclusions about comparative productivity.

Another feature of the agricultural sector which merits special attention in the context of productivity measurement is the role of inputs. It is a sector in which 'raw materials' such as feeding-stuffs, seeds and fertilisers, have a major impact on output and productivity levels. Whilst an appropriate allowance for these inputs, using double deflation techniques, is by no means straightfoward, happily it proves somewhat easier and more reliable than in other sectors. Consequently an adjustment has been made to the basic results.

In the case of this sector, data availability point to 1974 as the most appropriate base year for the productivity comparisons. The base year productivity ratios are carried backwards and forwards in the manner indicated in chapter 2.

MEASUREMENT OF AGRICULTURAL OUTPUT

Agricultural output was divided into three categories: meat products, other animal products and crops. Output of livestock was measured in tonnes of (dressed carcass) meat produced and unit values (price) based on this unit. Three types of meat were in turn distinguished, beef and veal, pork, and lamb and mutton. Inter-farm sales of livestock within each country have been excluded from the data. No account has been taken of the very small production of other meat (including horses) which in all three countries comprises less than 1 per cent of meat production.

Production of milk and eggs was measured by bulk weight, no allowance again being made for quality differences.[1] The price ratios for poultry meat, and thus the standardised gross output values, were derived from unit values, in turn obtained from tonnes of poultry meat and total values undistinguished as between chickens, turkeys, etc. There exist certain sundry items, such as wool, horsemeat, etc. which account for some 1 per cent or less of the total value of animal products in each country. Standardised gross output figures for this category are derived by deflating the appropriate country gross output values with the overall price ratio obtained for total animal products.

The output of crops is more diverse than in the case of animal products and the comparisons were based on volume and price data for 35 selected products. The most important output category in each country is feed and food grain[2] (wheat, barley, oats, rye, maize, rice and sorghum). For sorghum and maize, crops produced on any scale only in the United States, European shadow prices are employed, derived by assuming a price ratio (relative to the United States) based on that of the four common grains. The second category, major field crops, embraces only sugar beet in the case of the United Kingdom, and a small quantity of tobacco in West Germany. In the United States it comprises, additionally, the important crops, cotton, cottonseed, peanuts and soyabeans. For each of these commodities United States volumes and prices are derived in the same way as for the grains considered above. Again it is necessary to estimate a British shadow price for those crops not produced in the United Kingdom. In the case of cotton and tobacco it is preferable to use British import prices. For peanuts and soyabeans price ratios equal to the average for the category have been used. Output measurement for fruits and vegetables raises a problem which, though fairly common in productivity measurement generally, is rather less serious in the agricultural sector. In all three countries physical output data are available for almost all items but in the United Kingdom are accompanied by prices (and therefore implied gross values) for only a

[1] The manufacture of cheese and butter is excluded, these products being covered in the food manufacturing industry.

[2] Unlike Paige and Bombach (*A Comparison of National Output*) we have not excluded inter-farm sales of grain (for animal feed) and therefore this category figures more strongly than in their calculations.

few. Therefore, for this category, we have been obliged to base the comparisons on limited price data. For greenhouse and nursery products, legume and grass seeds, hops, mint, broomcorn, popcorn, hemp fibre and seeds, flax fibre, olives, tree nuts, hay and dried grass, maple syrup, flax seed, dry edible beans, dried peas and wine grapes we have obtained standardised gross output values by using the average price ratio for all crops.

THE LABOUR FORCE

Compared with output measurement in other sectors, that for agriculture proves to be comparatively straightforward. The opposite is true of the labour force, due to the participation of large numbers of self-employed, paid and unpaid family workers. Such groups are more difficult to quantify than wage and salary receiving employees, and their numbers are known with less accuracy and at fewer intervals in all three countries. An added complication is that comparable breakdowns of employment in the two sub-activities of the sector, forestry and fishing, appear to be unobtainable. Largely on this account, it proves impracticable to derive reliable comparative productivity ratios for forestry and fishing taken separately or as a single sub-sector.

In the case of the United Kingdom and United States the figures cited in table 8.2 for employment in this sector are taken from the ILO *Yearbook of Labour Statistics* and relate to 'total civilian employment' in 'agriculture, hunting, forestry and fishing'. In principle these series include employers, self-employed and unpaid family workers, as well as wage and salary earners. In fact the British figures do not appear to include unpaid family workers and whilst this will lend an upward bias to the United Kingdom labour productivity figure, the distortion will not be nearly so great as would result from a comparable treatment of the German agricultural labour force. A very high proportion of the sector's labour force in Germany is known to be part time (often female) workers. Consequently it was considered advisable to measure German agricultural labour input on a 'full time equivalent basis', using national sources,[1] and identifying a part-time worker as equivalent to half a full-time worker.[2]

[1] Statistisches Bundesamt, *Statistisches Jahrbuch Für Die Bundesrepublik Deutschland.*

[2] An attempt was made to compare British and German agricultural productivity using labour force data given in *EEC Agriculture and Food Statistics 1972–75*. This source reported a German agricultural labour force some 800 thousand below the level recorded by the ILO for the German agriculture, forestry and fishing sector. It is quite impossible that this number of workers was employed in forestry and fishing, so that we can only conclude that most were unpaid family workers in German agriculture. Consequently, the Germany/UK comparative agricultural productivity ratio based on these data emerges as about 0·90. This suggests an upper limit to the

COMPARATIVE PRODUCTIVITY IN AGRICULTURE, FORESTRY AND FISHING

In table 8.2 these labour force data are related to standardised net output data for the agriculture, forestry and fishing sectors to yield absolute and comparative labour productivity results. Standardised agricultural net outputs are obtained by deflating net outputs measured in domestic currencies by the relevant price ratios obtained for gross agricultural outputs. The same procedure is used to extend the comparison to forestry and fishing. Independent output measurement and comparisons in these activities proved impracticable and, as pointed out, estimation of separate labour force data was highly unreliable.

Table 8.2. *Comparative productivity in agriculture, forestry and fishing, 1974*

	United Kingdom			United States		Germany	
	£m	$m	DMm	£m	$m	£m	DMm
Standardised output							
Agriculture							
Gross output	4280	10820	31311	37069	86422	6051	44214
Input[a]	2611	6606	19100	18031	42036	3254	23778
Net output	1669	4214	12211	19038	44386	2797	20436
Subsidies, etc.[a]	262	663	1916	228	531	155	1131
Net output at factor cost	1931	4877	14127	19266	44917	2952	21567
Forestry and fishing net output[a]	136	344	996	1803	4200	586	4290
Total net output	2067	5221	15123	21069	49117	3538	25857
Labour force (thousands)		683[b]		3588		1573[c]	
	£	$	DM	£	$	£	DM
Output per man	3026	7644	22142	5872	13689	2249	16438
Comparative productivity (UK = 100)							
In UK prices	1·00			1·94		0·74	
In US/Germany prices		1·00	1·00		1·79		0·74

Sources: See text; ILO, *Yearbook of Labour Statistics*; *Statistiches Jahrbuch.*
[a] Deflated to a standardised basis by the appropriate price ratios for agricultural gross output.
[b] Excluding unpaid family workers.
[c] Full time equivalent.

DOUBLE DEFLATED RESULTS

It is thought that double deflation is especially important in the agricultural sector where international differences in raw material coefficients can exert a strong influence on labour productivity levels. In

Germany/UK ratio for agriculture and, by implication, for the whole agriculture, forestry and fishing sector.

Table 8.3. *Double deflated comparative productivity in agriculture, forestry and fishing, 1974*

	United Kingdom £m	United Kingdom $m	United Kingdom DMm	United States £m	United States $m	Germany £m	Germany DMm
Standardised output							
Agriculture							
Gross output	4280	10820	31311	37069	86422	6051	44214
Inputs double deflated	2611	6851	18520	16507	42036	3324	23778
Double deflated net output	1669	3969	12791	20562	44386	2727	20436
Subsidies, etc.[a]	262	624	2007	246	531	151	1131
Double deflated net output at factor cost	1931	4593	14798	20808	44917	2878	21567
Forestry and fishing double deflated net output	136	324	1042	1944	4200	573	4290
Total double deflated net output	2067	4917	15840	22752	49117	3451	25857
Labour force (thousands)		683[b]		3588		1573[c]	
	£	$	DM	£	$	£	DM
Double deflated net output per man	3026	7199	23192	6341	13689	2194	16438
Comparative productivity (UK = 100)							
In UK prices	1·00			2·10		0·73	
In US/Germany prices		1·00	1·00		1·90		0·71

Sources: Table 8.2; see also text.
[a] Deflated to a standardised basis by the price ratios implicit in double deflated agricultural net output.
[b] Excluding unpaid family workers.
[c] Full time equivalent.

particular, the amount of fertiliser used on a piece of land and the quantity and quality of food provided for animals will clearly have a direct and substantial impact on the *per capita* output of crops and cattle. Fortunately, whilst the quality of the data available on inputs, both prices and quantities, is inferior to agricultural output data, it is rather better than input data in other sectors, and adequate enough to encourage an attempt at double deflation.

In the first place, international price data are available for nitrogenous, phosphate and potash fertilisers, weighted by the quantities used in different countries.[1] This source yields price ratios for fertiliser and lime inputs.

Secondly, since the vast majority of agricultural inputs are supplied by the agriculture sector itself, some of the price ratios derived above for agricultural output are also relevant for inputs. Thus expenditures on feeding stuffs, imported livestock and seed have been deflated by the price ratios obtained, respectively, for grains, meat products and all crops. Clearly this is hardly an ideal procedure (for example, a sizeable component of feeding stuffs input will comprise *processed* feeding stuffs)

[1] United Nations Food and Agricultural Organisation, *Annual Yearbook, 1975*.

but it is considered preferable to a blanket application of gross output price ratios and sufficiently reliable to show, at least, the sensitivity of the comparative productivity results to double deflation.

For the two remaining categories, fuel and repairs and other expenses, neither independent price ratios nor relevant output price indices are available. For these categories the gross agricultural output price ratios were used. The results are set out in table 8.3.

CONTEMPORARY PRODUCTIVITY

In table 8.4 the productivity results obtained for 1974 are extended to earlier and later years. The sources drawn upon for this exercise are noted in the table. The results indicate that agricultural productivity and comparative productivity are subject to relatively pronounced annual fluctuations.

Table 8.4. *Comparative productivity in agriculture, forestry and fishing, 1968–77*

Year	Net output per head (£ per man, 1974 prices)			Comparative productivity (UK = 1·00)	
	UK	US	Germany	US/UK	Germany/UK
1968	2004	4821	1551	2·42	0·77
1969	2118	5236	1528	2·47	0·72
1970	2349	5637	1655	2·40	0·70
1971	2629	6039	1802	2·30	0·69
1972	2803	5812	1853	2·07	0·66
1973	2864	6037	2144	2·11	0·75
1974	3026	5872	2249	1·94	0·74
1975	2813	6231	2223	2·22	0·79
1976	2610	6080	2258	2·33	0·86
1977	3098	6471	2547	2·09	0·82

Sources: Table 8.2; UN, *Yearbook of National Accounts Statistics*; ILO, *Yearbook of Labour Statistics*; US, *Statistical Abstract.*

9

EXTRACTIVE INDUSTRIES

STRUCTURE OF THE INDUSTRY AND METHOD

Practical and methodological considerations eventually dictated that productivity comparisons for this sector be made for the three component industries shown in table 9.1: coal mining; petroleum and natural gas production; and the remaining activities – stone, slate, metalliferous and non-metalliferous mining and quarrying. The labour force data in this table record the sharp contrasts in the international make-up of this sector: the domination of coal mining in Britain, oil and gas in the United States and the comparative importance of the 'other' activities in Germany. What it fails to show is the vast increase in British oil and natural gas production in very recent years. Taking 1975 as 100, the British output index for this activity in 1978 was 30,954!

Table 9.1. *Employment structure of the extractive industries*[a]

	1967			1977		
	UK	US	Germany	UK	US	Germany
	Percentages					
Coal mining	89·3	23·2	51·7	85·7	26·2	49·3
Petroleum and natural gas	[b]	44·2	1·3	2·0	48·7	1·6
Other mining	10·7	32·6	47·0	12·3	25·1	49·1
Extractive industries	100·0	100·0	100·0	100·0	100·0	100·0

Sources: UK, *Annual Abstract of Statistics*; US, *Statistical Abstract*; Germany, *Statistisches Jahrbuch*.

[a] Employment data on which this table was based differ from those in table 9.2 partly because of differences in the years covered, and partly because of discrepancies between census and other national sources.

[b] Small number only.

Contemporary labour productivity comparisons have been made for two of the sector's three activities – coal mining, and oil and gas extraction – and the results carried back to earlier years using appropriate output and labour force indices. In the case of 'other' extractive activities, productivity comparisons based on the 1967/68 production censuses in the three countries have been brought forward to current years, again using appropriate output and employment indices. This latter procedure is also possible for coal mining and has been carried out for comparison with, and as a check on, the contemporary labour productivity results obtained for this activity.

COAL AND 'OTHER' MINING AND QUARRYING

Table 9.2 sets out the basic data – gross and net outputs together with employment – for coal mining and 'other' mining, taken from the American and German censuses of 1967 and the British 1968 census. The United States and German output data in this table are deflated by US/UK and Germany/UK price ratios relating to these two activities. The derivation of these price indices is based on the identification in the respective censuses of selected products for which sales values, quantities and thus average values can be obtained. For coal mining, a single product, coal, has sufficed. For the United States and Germany output and employment in open-cast mining are included in the comparison; in the United Kingdom this activity is classified with construction. In terms of coverage and bias in the comparative productivity measures, the discrepancy is of little import for, unlike the position in America and Germany, open-cast coal mining in the United Kingdom is on a very small scale. However, as an explanation of the coal mining productivity contrasts, this distinction is of considerable significance, for labour

Table 9.2. *Basic data for coal mining and 'other' mining, 1967–8*

	Coal mining	'Other' mining	Coal and 'other' mining[a]
Gross output			
UK (£m)	738	301	1040
US ($m)	3130	5605	8735
Germany (DMm)	10122	6070	16193
Net output			
UK (£m)	545	181	727
US ($m)	2091	3845	5936
Germany (DMm)	7407	3918	11325
Employment (thousands)			
UK	391	50	441
US	132	268	400
Germany	307	121	428

Sources: UK, *1968 Census of Production*; US, *1967 Census of Mineral Industries*; Germany, *Zensus im Produzierenden Gewerbe 1967*.

[a] i.e. extractive industries excluding oil and gas extraction.

Table 9.3. *Comparative productivity in coal mining and 'other' mining, 1967–8*

	Gross output		Net output	
	UK prices	US prices	UK prices	US prices
Comparative productivity US/UK (UK = 1·00)				
Coal mining	9·83	9·83	8·89	8·89
'Other' mining	1·77	1·56	2·02	1·78
Coal and 'other' mining	5·62	5·25	5·45	5·09
	UK prices	German prices	UK prices	German prices
Comparative productivity Germany/UK (UK = 1·00)				
Coal mining	1·91	1·91	1·89	1·89
'Other' mining	1·02	0·74	1·10	0·80
Coal and 'other' mining	1·83	1·63	1·82	1·64

Sources: See table 9.2 and text.

productivity in open-cast mining is likely to be substantially better than in deep mines.

In the case of the US/UK comparison for 'other' mining, selected product coverage and therefore reliability of the results is poor. Coverage, by nine products, is better for the Germany/UK comparison. Even in this case, however, German coverage is significantly less than British. This reflects the fact that in the German census of production, the quarrying and extraction of stone, slate, sand, chalk, clay, limestone, etc. is classified as a manufacturing activity and included with subsequent processing activities. Since the actual quarrying and extraction could not be separated from these processing activities to correspond with the British classification, all these German activities, extraction and processing, were transferred from the manufacturing sector to mining and quarrying. Consequently much of the total German sales and output data refer to semi-finished or finished products yielding a relatively low coverage by selected products as a percentage of total sales.

The results, set out in table 9.3, reveal that in the case of coal mining the US/UK productivity ratio was 8·89 in 1967–8 and the Germany/UK ratio 1·89. When these are brought forward to 1977, by appropriate productivity indices for the three countries, the results suggest comparative productivity ratios of, respectively, 7·93 and 2·50. These estimates can, in turn, be compared with ratios obtained directly for 1977 from coal output in tonnes and employment, 7·60 and 2·64. The results are reassuringly close, and it matters little which are adopted when calculating the sector's aggregate productivity ratios. Those based on direct measurement were in the event used.

OIL AND GAS EXTRACTION

Whilst output of both oil and natural gas is well documented in all three countries, only in the United States can the labour force be apportioned between oil production and natural gas extraction. Thus it was necessary in the United Kingdom and Germany (and therefore in the United States) to express the output of this sector in terms of a single unit, tonnes of oil equivalent, and to relate this to the relevant employment levels. Ideally, and in conformity with the general methodological principle adopted in this study, the conversion of natural gas (and natural gas liquids) to oil equivalents should be based on relative prices. A scarcity of reliable relative price data in the three countries – to say nothing of the extent to which relative oil and gas prices have changed in recent years – precludes this approach. Instead, conversion to tonnes of

Table 9.4. *Comparative productivity in oil and natural gas extraction, 1977*

	Oil equivalent (m tonnes)	Labour (th)	Output per man (tonnes)	Comparative productivity (UK = 1·00)
UK	73·5	7	10500	1·00
US	939·6	405	2320	0·22
Germany	21·7	6·5	3338	0·32

Sources: UK, Department of Energy, *Digest of United Kingdom Energy Statistics* and *Annual Abstract of Statistics*; US, *Statistical Abstract*; Germany, *Statistisches Jahrbuch.*

oil equivalent has been effected using physical coefficients. The results are set out in table 9.4.

AGGREGATION OF SUB-SECTOR RATIOS

From the previous sections have emerged US/UK comparative productivity ratios for 1977 of 7·60, 0·22 and 1·82[1] for coal mining, oil and natural gas, and 'other' mining, respectively. In the case of the Germany/UK comparisons, the ratios are 2·64, 0·32 and 1·40. Derivation of an aggregate comparative US/UK and Germany/UK productivity ratio for the whole extractive industry sector must take account not only of the ratios of these component activities but also of variations between these sub-sectors in (value of) net output per head.

Difficulties arise because of a scarcity of net output value data for 1977, the year for which, in the case of this sector, the aggregation must

[1] When the results for this sector in 1967–8 (given in table 9.3) are brought forward with suitable indices.

be undertaken. The information we possess comprises: employment and value of net output for the three sub-sectors taken from the British production census of 1977, together with 1977 sub-sector comparative productivity ratios. In these circumstances, the reverse valuation technique described in the Technical Note has been used to aggregate the sub-sector ratios into comparative productivity measures for the whole extractive industry sector. The procedure yields, for 1977, a US/UK ratio of 3·42 and a Germany/UK ratio of 1·51.

COMPARATIVE PRODUCTIVITY IN EARLIER YEARS

The results obtained for 1977 have been taken back to other years (table 9.5) by the customary procedure. That is, (standardised) net output and employment levels have been carried back by means of official (real) output indices and employment series. The output of British oil and gas has not been taken back further than 1976. Some production did occur prior to that year but the official output index behaves in a highly erratic fashion.

Table 9.5. *Comparative productivity in extractive industries, 1968–77*

UK = 1·00

Year	Coal mining	Oil and natural gas	'Other' mining	Extractive industries
US/UK comparison				
1968	8·55		2·08	6·68
1969	8·81		1·88	6·65
1970	8·92		1·86	6·92
1971	8·43		1·87	6·84
1972	10·38		1·82	8·06
1973	8·16		1·61	6·64
1974	8·69		1·60	6·91
1975	6·97		1·67	5·94
1976	7·18	0·69	1·91	4·84
1977	7·60	0·22	1·82	3·42
Germany/UK comparison				
1968	2·23		1·19	2·00
1969	2·33		1·15	2·08
1970	2·33		1·16	2·13
1971	2·29		1·16	2·12
1972	2·92		1·11	2·55
1973	2·62		0·95	2·25
1974	3·01		1·00	2·54
1975	2·52		1·14	2·32
1976	2·68	0·90	1·21	1·97
1977	2·64	0·32	1·40	1·51

Sources: See tables 9.3 and 9.4, and text; UK, *Annual Abstract of Statistics*, US, *Statistical Abstract*; Germany, *Statistiches Jahrbuch*.

10

MANUFACTURING INDUSTRY

For some sectoral productivity comparisons the methodology outlined in chapter 2 needs significant modification. In the case of manufacturing it can be applied with little change. However data deficiencies in recent censuses prevent the direct measurement of manufacturing productivity for a contemporary year. In the first instance, therefore, manufacturing industry productivity comparisons have been made for 1967–8: major American and German production censuses were undertaken in 1967 and a British one in 1968. The productivity differentials which emerge for this period are then moved forwards in time by industry output and employment indices.

COMPARATIVE US/UK PRODUCTIVITY RATIOS, 1967–8

The first step in the industry productivity comparison comprises an industry identification process: an alignment of the relevant American activities, at the four-digit level of the United States 1967 Standard Industrial Classification (SIC), with the corresponding British activity at the Minimum List Heading (MLH) level of the United Kingdom 1968 SIC. An attempt has been made to adhere consistently to certain principles when effecting these identifications. In particular efforts were made to avoid combining British MLHs in an attempt to provide a sufficient number of industry readings for analytical purposes. Inevitably, in order to ensure a 'match' with corresponding American activities, the principle was on occasion breached, though this was to some extent balanced by certain subdivisions of MLHs which proved possible. Secondly, MLHs were transferred from one 'Order' to another only when a satisfactory correspondence with American activities could be achieved by no other means. Thirdly, the industry identification is exhaustive in the sense that for both the United Kingdom and United States all manufacturing activities have been embraced. This means that manufacturing activities which are found only in one of the two countries must be allocated to some industry that has been 'matched'. This is required only infrequently and in practice poses few problems; usually there is little doubt about the industry to which the activity in question is most akin. Application of these principles yields, in the case of the US/UK comparison, productivity measures for 117 component manufacturing industries.

There is a preference in productivity comparisons for industry net outputs to be valued at factor cost rather than market prices. Factor cost valuation is appropriate because productivity comparisons are eventually concerned with individual factors of production. Aggregation of sectoral productivity relatives, requiring value added per man, could yield misleading results if based on market price, rather than factor cost, valuations.[1] It proves possible to work with the factor cost output concept in the case of both British and American censuses. In the British census a figure for excise taxes paid (or any subsidies received) is provided so that any gross and net outputs at market prices may be converted to a factor cost basis for comparison with the United States.

The 1968 British census of production gives figures of the numbers employed on average during the year, inclusive and exclusive of working proprietors, and apportions head office staff among the various plants. In the United States apparently no efforts are made to allocate head office staff among the four-digit level industries but such data are provided at the United States two-digit SIC level, equivalent to United Kingdom 'Orders'. These data have been used to make estimates of the American industries' labour forces inclusive of headquarters staff, to promote a greater degree of consistency with the British employment data.[2]

Derivation of international price ratios from the average values of selected products in the census reports is a crucial element in the procedure adopted in this report for manufacturing productivity measurement. The foundation of the method, its strength and weaknesses and the degree of judgement involved in the selection and matching of the products on which the ratios are based, have been noted in chapter 2. A complexity arises because although prices derived from the American census accord with the American factor cost output valuations, those derived from the British census are market prices (i.e. including excise taxes) and these do not accord with British output figures adjusted to factor cost valuations. Thus in some industries where British indirect taxes (or subsidies) are significant, deflation of British and American factor cost output data by means of census derived price ratios would yield biased results. Census price ratios were accordingly

[1] See Technical Note.

[2] United States census information about numbers of head office personnel employed at the three-digit SIC level, corresponding approximately to the United Kingdom MLH level, is available. Whilst these data are provided on an enterprise rather than a plant basis, they can be used to indicate in which of our industries the estimation procedure described above might be misleading. This check has been made and the results taken into account when the reliability of the various industry results is gauged.

adjusted in these cases. Price ratios so obtained are used to 'standardise' United States net output values in £ sterling, from which comparative productivity levels are then derived. This method has been used for the bulk of the industry comparisons. In those cases where it is not employed the principal alternative is the introduction of non-census price ratios (or, very occasionally, the use of input indicators).

COMPARATIVE GERMANY/UK PRODUCTIVITY RATIOS, 1967–8

Individual German manufacturing industries (as defined in the 'Systematik der Wirtschaftszweige') were aligned in as much detail as possible with corresponding activities in the United Kingdom at the Minimum List Heading level of the 1968 SIC. The identification principles followed in the case of the US/UK comparison were also adopted for the Germany/UK comparison. In Germany some activities classified in the census under 'manufacturing' belong to other sectors in the United Kingdom. Examples include the construction of bridges from steel and light metal and some municipal engineering which, though part of the iron and steel industry in Germany, is regarded as a construction activity in the United Kingdom. There are also some activities in the German census of manufactures which in the United Kingdom are classified under distributive trades or services. These have been omitted from the manufacturing comparison. The matching procedure yielded 69 component manufacturing industries.

In the UK/US comparison efforts were made to produce sectoral net outputs and contributions to GDP valued at factor cost *not* market prices. This has been impossible in the case of the 1967 German census data. Basically, in the German census gross output is valued at market prices (though production for stocks and self-produced equipment is valued at production cost) so that net output includes indirect taxes and excludes subsidies, yielding effectively a market price valuation. Since separate figures for excise taxes paid or subsidies received are not readily available in Germany, net output has been compared with British data on a similar, market price, basis.

The German census provides figures of numbers of people employed at the enterprise or plant level. Employment statistics at enterprise level have been used since they include head office staff; working proprietors have been embraced throughout.

As in the US/UK comparisons, the bulk of the industry productivity comparisons are based on census price ratios. It has, however, been necessary in a few cases to use price ratios derived from Kravis *et al.*[1]

[1] *A System of International Comparisons.*

Table 10.1. *Comparative productivity in manufacturing industries, US/UK 1967–8*

SIC Order[a]	Industry	Net output per man UK £	Net output per man US[b] £	Comparative productivity UK = 1·00	Reliability assessment[c]
1	Grain milling	4047	11268	2·78	3
2	Bread and flour confectionery	1355	2861	2·11	2
3	Biscuits	1579	5519	3·50	3
4	Bacon curing, meal and fish products	1671	4063	2·43	2
5	Milk and milk products	2033	3557	1·75	1
6	Sugar	3013	5022	1·67	1
7	Cocoa, chocolate and sugar confectionery	1782	5562	3·12	4
8	Fruit and vegetable products	2008	4868	2·42	4
9	Animal and poultry foods	3140	8866	2·82	1
10	Vegetable, animal oils and fats	3011	8020	2·66	2
11	Margarine	1707	6968	4·08	2
12	Starch and miscellaneous foods	3043	11499	3·78	2
13	Brewing and malting	3648	10098	2·77	3
14	Soft drinks	2054	4027	1·96	4
15	Other drink industries	4971	22712	4·57	2
16	Tobacco	3885	14253	3·67	2
III	Food, drink and tobacco	2323	5914	2·55	
17	Mineral oil refining	6368	14296	2·24	3
18	Lubricating oils and greases	3757	7422	1·98	3
IV	Petroleum products	5610	13858	2·47	
19	General chemicals	3702	10923	2·95	1
20	Pharmaceuticals	3501	11384	3·25	4
21	Toilet preparations	2970	11474	3·86	4
22	Paint	2608	6750	2·59	1
23	Soap and detergents	3775	10371	2·75	2
24	Plastics, synthetics	3464	7495	2·16	1
25	Fertilisers	3679	6629	1·80	2
26	Other chemicals	2491	8128	3·26	4
V	Chemicals and allied industries	3360	9608	2·86	
27	Iron, steel, coke ovens	2015	5185	2·57	1
28	Steel tubes	2022	5618	2·78	4
29	Iron castings	1658	3455	2·09	4
30	Aluminium	1780	6859	3·85	1
31	Copper	2241	5509	2·46	2
32	Other base metals	2741	5158	1·88	2
VI	Metal manufacture	1979	5174	2·61	
33	Agricultural machinery including tractors	2361	3797	1·61	2
34	Machine and engineers tools	1817	3330	1·83	2
35	Pumps and valves	1897	4500	2·37	3
36	Industrial engines	1899	11534	6·07	3
37	Textile machinery	1933	6107	3·16	3
38	Construction and earth moving equipment	2523	5569	2·21	4
39	Mechanical handling equipment	2141	6481	3·03	2
40	Office machinery	1948	6436	3·30	4
41	Mining machinery	1951	2702	1·38	3

Table 10.1 (*contd.*)

SIC Order[a]		Industry	Net output per man UK £	Net output per man US[b] £	Comparative productivity UK = 1·00	Reliability assessment[c]
42		Printing etc. machinery	1753	5235	2·99	3
43		Commercial fridges and space heaters	2044	3924	1·92	3
44		Food processing machinery	1860	6520	3·51	3
45		Non electrical machinery	2102	4146	1·97	3
46		Industrial plant	2306	3546	1·54	3
47		Ordnance and small arms	1722	3222	1·87	4
48		Mechanical engineering n.e.s.	1772	3954	2·23	4
	VII	Mechanical engineering	2008	4532	2·26	
49		Photographic equipment and materials	2129	10987	5·16	2
50		Watches and clocks	1282	4648	3·63	4
51		Surgical instruments and appliances	1677	5378	3·21	3
52		Scientific instruments	1818	5536	3·05	4
	VIII	Instrument engineering	1797	6581	3·66	
53		Electrical machinery	1866	5055	2·71	4
54		Telegraph and telephone apparatus	1589	4905	3·09	4
55		Radio and electronic components	1713	3502	2·04	2
56		Broadcasting equipment	1839	5465	2·97	2
57		Electronic computers	2403	7180	2·99	4
58		Electronic capital goods misc.	1815	5025	2.77	4
59		Domestic electrical appliances	1838	4475	2·43	2
	IX	Electrical engineering	1803	4789	2·66	
60	X	Shipbuilding and marine engineering	1461	2751	1·88	4
61		Motor vehicle manufacture	2069	9428	4·56	4
62		Motor cycle, cycle manufacture	1362	3622	2·66	2
63		Aerospace equipment	2020	8149	4·03	4
64		Locomotives etc.	1161	7764	6·69	4
	XI	Vehicles	1978	8736	4.42	
65		Hand tools and implements	1406	6143	4·37	3
66		Cutlery etc.	2335	2661	1·14	3
67		Bolts, nuts etc.	1587	4149	2·61	2
68		Wire and insulated cables	1996	5557	2·78	3
69		Cans and metal boxes	1457	6791	4·66	2
70		Iron and steel forgings	1759	4211	2·39	2
71		Vats, tanks, cisterns etc.	1700	4706	2·77	4
72		Jewellery and miscellaneous	1728	3876	2·24	4
	XII	Metal goods n.e.s.	1758	4411	2·51	
73		Manmade fibres	4045	7942	1·96	1
74		Spinning and doubling	1325	2721	2·05	1
75		Weaving	1267	2969	2·34	3
76		Woollen worsted	1415	2983	2·11	2
77		Jute and other textiles	1511	4108	2·72	4
78		Rope, twine, net	1348	2552	1·89	2
79		Hosiery and other knitted	1474	3327	2·26	1
80		Lace	1393	2745	1·97	4
81		Carpets	1730	4402	2·54	2
82		Narrow fabrics	1306	3465	2·65	2
83		Bedding and household textiles	1391	3471	2·50	2
84		Canvas goods and sacks	1260	3300	2·62	4
85		Textile finishing	1478	3593	2·43	4
86		Asbestos	1937	4137	2·14	3

Table 10.1 (*contd.*)

SIC Order[a]	Industry	Net output per man UK £	Net output per man US[b] £	Comparative productivity UK = 1·00	Reliability assessment[c]
XIII	Textiles	1593	3608	2·26	
87	Leather	1835	3943	2·15	2
88	Leather goods	1101	2348	2·13	2
89	Fur	1588	4563	2·87	4
XIV	Leather, leather goods, fur	1508	2936	1·95	
90	Weatherproof outerwear	1083	2275	2·10	2
91	Mens' and boys' outerwear	954	2195	2·30	1
92	Womens' and infants' clothing etc.	1094	2565	2·34	1
93	Overalls, shirts	929	2741	2·95	1
94	Hats, caps, millinery	1045	3508	3·36	1
95	Gloves	958	1122	1·17	1
96	Footwear	1305	2315	1·77	1
XV	Clothing and footwear	1088	2466	2·27	
97	Bricks, fireclay, refractory goods	1779	2998	1·69	3
98	Pottery	1201	1791	1·49	3
99	Glass	1908	4366	2·29	1
100	Cement	3504	6708	1·91	1
101	Abrasives and miscellaneous building materials	2327	3853	1·66	2
XVI	Bricks, pottery, glass, cement	1957	3880	1·98	
102	Timber	1820	7549	4·15	2
103	Furniture and office fittings	1804	4558	2·53	4
104	Wood containers and baskets	1404	6325	4·50	4
105	Miscellaneous wood and cork manufactures	1446	2203	1·52	3
XVII	Timber, furniture etc.	1754	5887	3·36	
106	Paper and board	2237	6962	3·11	1
107	Packaging products	1658	4859	2·93	1
108	Stationery and miscellaneous products	1965	6367	3·24	2
109	Newspapers and periodicals	2605	3451	1·32	3
110	Other printing	1817	2913	1·60	3
XVIII	Paper, printing, publishing	2050	4237	2·07	
111	Rubber	2089	4789	2·29	2
112	Linoleum	2220	5672	2·55	3
113	Brushes and brooms	1299	4023	3·10	2
114	Toys and games	1442	4997	3·47	3
115	Miscellaneous stationery goods	2214	3966	1·79	2
116	Plastic products	1796	5561	3·10	2
117	Miscellaneous manufacturing industries	1429	6226	4·36	3
XIX	Other manufacturing industries	1855	5582	3·01	
	All manufacturing	1953	5387	2·76	

[a] Approximate
[b] United Kingdom price weights
[c] (1) Good; (2) Reasonable; (3) Poor; (4) External data used; see text

Additionally in a few industries it was felt that the productivity differential based on gross outputs was more realistic than that derived from a net output comparison.

RELIABILITY OF THE RESULTS

Whilst, for comprehensive coverage, a comparative productivity figure must be calculated for all component industries of the manufacturing sector, only the more reliable industry productivity ratios have been subject to certain of the analyses of chapter 6. For this reason, and to gauge the overall accuracy of the picture portrayed for the manufacturing sector, it proved necessary to assess the reliability of the results obtained for each industry. Only occasionally has the reliability assessment been influenced by aspects of the calculations other than price ratios. There are isolated cases, such as petroleum refining, where misgivings about basic output or raw material valuations contributed to the final assessment. The degree of estimation involved in any adjustment for indirect taxes is also taken into account. In some industries, as explained above, the United States employment figures, and thus the comparative productivity results, may be subject to error.

Certain specific criteria are available for judging the census price ratios, on which the reliability of the productivity comparisons mainly hinges. Other things being equal, the larger the number of selected products and the greater the output coverage which they represent – both measurable characteristics – the more reliable should be the result.

Largely, though not entirely, on these bases, component industry productivity ratios were allocated to four categories. Typically an output coverage of the order of 80 per cent achieved by, say, some half dozen selected products, should confer high reliability and classification of the industry in the first category. The second group, for reasonably reliable results, embraces those industries where the product coverage is somewhat lower but where, again, there are a number of selected items.[1] The third and fourth categories embrace the least reliable results which have not been the subject of detailed scrutiny in chapter 6. The third group contains industries where product coverage is especially low, say less than 20 per cent, even when it reflects a fair number of selected products. The fourth is reserved essentially for those cases where price ratios could

[1] There is in effect a trade-off relationship when determining reliability between coverage and number of selected products. Industries where the coverage is no greater than some 30 per cent might still be included in the second category if there is a fair number of selected products, on the sampling theory principle that the resulting price ratios have a greater chance of approximating the actual ratio than the same coverage achieved by no more than one or two selected items.

Table 10.2. *Comparative productivity in manufacturing industries, Germany/UK 1967–8*

SIC Order[a]		Industry	Net output per man UK £	Net output per man Germany[b] £	Comparative productivity UK = 1·00	Reliability assessment[c]
1		Grain milling	4047	2670	0·66	2
2		Bread and flour confectionery	1355	1263	0·93	4
3		Biscuits	1579	1299	0·82	2
4		Bacon curing, meat and fish products	1557	1408	0·90	2
5		Milk and milk products	2033	2450	1·21	2
6		Sugar	6293	3090	0·49	1
7		Cocoa, chocolate and sugar confectionery	1772	1917	1·08	2
8		Fruit and vegetable products, soft drinks; starch and miscellaneous foods	2261	2459	1·09	2
9		Animal and poultry foods	3140	4615	1·47	3
10		Vegetable and animal fats; margarine	2597	4728	1·82	1
11		Brewing and malting	8404	8777	1·04	1
12		Other drink industries	13346	14013	1·05	2
13		Tobacco	30120	34351	1·14	2
	III	Food, drink and tobacco	4461	4128	0·93	4
14		Coke ovens and manufactured fuels	2670	2690	1·01	4
15		Mineral oil refining; lubricating oils and greases	6153	6953	1·13	3
	IV	Coal and petroleum products	4697	6455	1·37	
16	V	Chemicals and allied industries; man-made fibres	3371	4614	1·38	2
17		Iron and steel; steel tubes; wire and wire manufactures	1966	2982	1·52	1
18		Iron castings	1658	1816	1·10	3
19		Aluminium; copper, brass and other copper alloys; other base metals	2131	2419	1·14	1
	VI	Metal manufacture	1950	2702	1·39	1
20		Agricultural machinery including tractors	2361	2915	1·23	2
21		Metal working machine tools	1897	2600	1·37	4
22		Construction and earth-moving equipment; mechanical handling equipment; mining machinery; industrial plant and steelwork	2272	2326	1·02	4
23		Office machinery	1948	3594	1·84	4
24		Printing, book-binding etc. machinery	1753	3075	1·75	4
25		Space-heating, ventilating and airconditioning equipment	2015	2311	1·15	4
26		Ordnance and small arms	1722	2059	1·20	4
27		Other machinery	1939	2510	1·29	4
28		Other mechanical engineering n.e.s.	1772	2430	1·37	4
	VII	Mechanical engineering	2011	2581	1·28	
29		Photographic and scientific instruments	1843	1917	1·04	3
30		Watches and clocks	1282	1665	1·30	4

Table 10.2 (*contd.*)

SIC	Order[a]	Industry	Net output per man UK £	Net output per man Germany[b] £	Comparative productivity UK = 1·00	Reliability assessment[c]
31		Surgical instruments and appliances	1498	2014	1·34	3
	VIII	Instrument engineering	1748	1900	1·09	
32	IX	Electrical engineering	1826	1710	0·94	2
33	X	Shipbuilding and marine engineering	1461	1421	0·97	2
34		Motor vehicle manufacturing; motor cycle, tricycle etc. manufacturing	2042	2869	1·42	4
35		Aerospace equipment	2020	2287	1·13	4
36		Railway carriages, wagons and trams	1196	1899	1·59	2
	XI	Vehicles	1998	2808	1·41	
37		Engineers small tools	1658	2282	1·37	4
38		Cutlery and tableware	2335	1853	0·79	2
39		Jewellery and precious metals	2317	2006	0·87	4
40		Metal industries n.e.s.	1664	2200	1·32	2
	XII	Metal goods n.e.s.	1709	2183	1·28	
41		Spinning and doubling	1325	1798	1·36	4
42		Weaving of cotton and linen	1267	1925	1·52	2
43		Woollen and worsted	1415	1675	1·18	2
44		Jute and canvas	1228	1819	1·48	3
45		Hosiery and other knitted goods	1474	1351	0·92	2
46		Textile finishing	1478	1910	1·29	4
47		Bedding and soft furnishings	1746	1631	0·93	3
48		Other textiles	1612	2126	1·32	2
	XIII	Textiles	1434	1748	1·22	
49		Leather	1835	1830	1·00	2
50		Leather goods	1101	1475	1·34	4
51		Fur	1588	1752	1·10	4
	XIV	Leather, leather goods, fur	1508	1626	1·08	
52		Clothing	1030	1051	1·02	1
53		Footwear	1305	1113	0·85	2
	XV	Clothing and footwear	1087	1062	0·98	
54		Bricks, fireclay and refractory goods	1779	3720	2·09	1
55		Pottery and abrasives	1386	1533	1·11	3
56		Glass	1908	2698	1·41	2
57		Cement	3504	5260	1·50	1
58		Building materials n.e.s.	2292	4052	1·77	2
	XVI	Bricks, pottery, glass, cement	1957	3153	1·61	
59		Timber	1820	2350	1·29	2
60		Furniture and office fittings	1804	3505	1·94	4
61		Wooden containers and baskets; brushes and brooms	1363	2959	2·17	3
62		Miscellaneous wood and cork manufactures	1446	1229	0·85	3
	XVII	Timber, furniture etc.	1735	2773	1·60	
63		Paper and board products	1934	3152	1·63	1
64		Printing and publishing	2127	2728	1·28	4
	XVIII	Paper, printing, publishing	2050	3075	1·50	
65		Rubber and asbestos	2067	2031	0·98	2
66		Floor coverings and plastic products	1860	2458	1·32	3

Table 10.2 (*contd.*)

SIC Order[a]		Industry	Net output per man UK £	Net output per man Germany[b] £	Comparative productivity UK = 1·00	Reliability assessment[c]
67		Toys and games	1442	1455	1·01	3
68		Miscellaneous stationers' goods	2214	3327	1·50	3
69		Miscellaneous manufacturing industries	1429	1203	0·84	3
	XIX	Other manufacturing industries	1877	2122	1·13	
		All manufacturing	2173	2678	1·23	

[a] Approximate
[b] United Kingdom price weights
[c] (1) Good; (2) Reasonable; (3) Poor; (4) External data used; see text

not be derived from census data, so that combined Order price ratios, external price ratios or other strategems were used.

In the case of the overall US/UK manufacturing comparison, the results are based on almost 500 selected products; in the case of the Germany/UK comparison, on some 350.

In addition to the individual industry results, comparative productivity ratios have been calculated at the level of United Kingdom SIC Orders, or approximations thereto, in both the US/UK and Germany/UK comparisons.[1] For this purpose, the standardised output figures for the component industries within an Order are summed and divided by the appropriate Order employment figures, the procedure described in chapter 2. By the same means, a productivity comparison for the manufacturing sector as a whole has been derived from the Order productivity data. The results of the US/UK comparison are set out in table 10.1 and for the Germany/UK comparison in table 10.2.

DOUBLE DEFLATED RESULTS[2]

An attempt was made to obtain, for the US/UK comparison, double deflated manufacturing productivity ratios by two routes. The first related to the overall result for the sector, the second to individual industries.

The procedures described above yield a US/UK price ratio for the outputs of each component manufacturing industry. Suitably weighted,

[1] As noted previously, it occasionally proved necessary for industry identification purposes to transfer MLHs, or parts of MLHs, to Orders in which they are not normally found.
[2] For a description of this technique and its relevance to the study see chapter 2 and Technical Note.

these ratios produce a price index for inputs into the manufacturing sector derived from manufacturing activities. Such an index was obtained using as weights the manufacturing sector's purchases from individual industries as shown in the British 1968 Input-Output tables.[1] The resulting price index was used to standardise in £ sterling purchases of inputs by the United States manufacturing sector. This figure is in turn deducted from standardised United States gross output figures to yield a double deflated value of net output. A comparison of American and British productivity on this basis yields a ratio of 2·95 compared with the unadjusted (United States weighted) ratio of 2·52.

For the second approach, fourteen manufacturing industries (out of those with comparatively reliable unadjusted productivity ratios) were selected on the grounds that some 25 per cent or more of raw material inputs in both countries could be covered by a US/UK price index. When the double deflation technique is applied to this group of industries an unadjusted productivity ratio of 2·63, on British prices, is reduced to 1·99, and an unadjusted ratio of 2·53 on American prices is reduced to 1·83. However, the impact is far from consistent between the fourteen industries and in general – for reasons considered in chapters 2, 3 and the Technical Note – the results inspire little confidence.

CONTEMPORARY PRODUCTIVITY

Because of census of production deficiencies, it was found impracticable to make labour productivity comparisons between British, American and German manufacturing industries for a recent year. This deficiency has been remedied by 'moving' forward the labour productivity results obtained for these three countries in 1967–8, with the help of appropriate (real) output and labour force indices for the British, American and German manufacturing industries.

Table 10.3 sets out the results of the exercise. For each country the base year manufacturing census net output figure has been projected by the official index of changes in manufacturing output to yield net output values, standardised in 1968 pounds sterling, for recent years. The labour force series have been compiled in similar fashion, the base year (1967 or 1968) census employment figure is projected by an official labour force series for manufacturing. The census labour force figures in all three countries embrace employees and working proprietors but not the self-employed. To achieve maximum consistency, therefore, the base year census employment figure has been projected by official series of

[1] CSO, *Input-Output Tables for the United Kingdom, 1968*, Studies in Official Statistics No 22, HMSO 1973. The method implicitly assumes that the American pattern of manufacturing sector inputs from other manufacturing industries is the same as Britain's.

Table 10.3. *Comparative productivity in the manufacturing sector, 1968–77*

Year	Net output per head				Comparative productivity (UK = 1·00)	
	US/UK comparison		Germany/UK comparison			
	UK[a]	US	UK[a]	Germany	US/UK	Germany/UK
	(£ per man, 1968 prices)					
1968	1953	5651	2173	2935	2·89	1·35
1969	1998	5781	2223	3103	2·89	1·40
1970	2010	5733	2236	3019	2·85	1·35
1971	2061	6052	2293	3050	2·94	1·33
1972	2200	6440	2447	3199	2·93	1·31
1973	2367	6639	2633	3517	2·80	1·34
1974	2316	6196	2576	3515	2·68	1·36
1975	2282	6432	2553	3573	2·82	1·40
1976	2398	6806	2668	3918	2·84	1·47
1977	2403	6986	2673	4069	2·91	1·52

Sources: See tables 10.1 and 10.2, and text; UK, *Annual Abstract of Statistics* and *National Income and Expenditure*; US, *Monthly Labor Review* and *Statistical Abstract*; Germany, Statistisches Bundesamt, *Lange Reihen zur Wirtschaftsentwicklung* and *Statistisches Jahrbuch.*
[a] For difference see text

employees in manufacturing. A shortcoming of the German series is that it is based on plants with more than 10 employees.

Table 5.4 presents contemporary US/UK and Germany/UK comparative productivity ratios for twelve component manufacturing industries. It will be recalled that productivity ratios were calculated for 117 component industries in the case of the US/UK 1967–8 comparisons and for 69 industries for the Germany/UK 1967–8 comparisons. Since real output indices are not readily available at such a fine level from American and German sources, it proved necessary to calculate contemporary component productivity levels at, essentially, the UK Order level.

To obtain the original US/UK and Germany/UK industry identifications, it was necessary to switch certain American and German manufacturing activities. This means that some relatively unimportant inconsistencies arise, in the case of both the German and American data, as a result of applying inter-temporal indices to base year output and employment figures with which they do not wholly match. However, the effect of such inconsistencies is limited by working at Order level. The output indices used for these twelve manufacturing industries are based on official production indices for individual industries.

11

THE CONSTRUCTION INDUSTRY

STRUCTURE OF THE INDUSTRY

Two basic features of construction activity which dominate and complicate any productivity comparison are the wide range of outputs for which the industry is responsible and the lack of homegeneity which typically characterises each type of output. The end products of construction activity range from a bridge to the decoration of a house and no two bridges or house decorations may be the same. The second feature is that the gestation period of the bulk of the industry's output – especially of building and civil engineering projects – is long. Many projects require more than twelve months and the amount of work which spans two annual periods – a kind of work in progress – is high relative to annual output.

Consequently, data relating to the annual value of project starts (frequently available from issues of building and construction permits) or of project completions, may be poor measures of work done in a given year. In fact, in all three countries, census questionnaires seek to obtain a gross output figure for the sector which approximates work done.

Whether measured by gross output, net output, or employment, building activity appears to bulk larger than civil engineering. On a net output basis, these two sub-sectors account for 68 per cent of construction activity in the United Kingdom and 54 per cent in the United States. The corresponding proportion in Germany, where no division between building and civil engineering seems practicable, lies between these, 62 per cent. Correspondingly, specialised construction trades account for an appreciably greater proportion of the sector's activity in the United States than in either Germany or the United Kingdom.

MEASURING COMPARATIVE PRODUCTIVITY IN CONSTRUCTION

Measures of comparative productivity based directly on physical units of output are entirely impracticable for the construction industry. Were different kinds of construction output – houses, apartments, hotels, hospitals, schools, roads, bridges, tunnels, dams, etc – the sole and exclusive output of separately defined sub-sectors of construction, then a measure of physical output per man might be practicable for one or two sub-sectors. In such a situation, the number of three bedroomed houses per man, or number of apartments per man, might be measured and roughly compared. Even in these hypothetical circumstances, however, such physical comparisons would be the exception not the rule. As previously stated, there is a lack of homogeneity in units of output even within each range of construction activity; rarely are two hospitals, schools, tunnels, bridges, etc alike. And even in the case of residential buildings for which, in the circumstances specified, such a physical approach might just conceivably be practicable, variations in housing types within and between countries would render the exercise at best very complex and unreliable.

In practice it is not possible to identify a series of such sub-sectors responsible for specific outputs. Work performed on hospital construction will reflect the activities of a general building establishment, perhaps some civil engineering undertakings and certainly some of the specialised trades, and similarly with other outputs of the sector.

In brief, in this sector we merely have, on one side of the productivity equation, a series of values of the amount of construction of residential buildings, hospitals, roads, bridges, etc, and on the other a total labour force which cannot be allocated to the individual outputs.[1] In these circumstances the best available method of deriving a productivity measure, comparable across countries, lies in deflating the output values of the industry in the three countries to a common currency basis, as a prelude to calculating and comparing (standardised) output per man. Fortunately, the international price data collected by Kravis *et al.*[2] enables this approach to be pursued.

COMPARATIVE PRODUCTIVITY

The availability of construction industry censuses, containing net output and labour force data, determine the base years for the productivity comparison. A US/UK and Germany/UK comparison was made for 1967–8 using the American and German censuses for 1967 and the British one for 1968. The relevant data are set out in table 11.1 which constitutes the basis for the productivity comparison. The British data include opencast coal mining and hire of construction plant, both of which are regarded as construction activities in the UK. In 1976, the former accounted for some 0·6 per cent of the British industry's output and 0·4 per cent of employment, the latter 5·2 per cent and 3·5 per cent

[1] Frequently – though not in the case of the United States – census returns also fail to itemise, separately, amount of work by type – houses, bridges, etc.

[2] Kravis *et al.*, 1975.

Table 11.1. *Construction industry basic data, 1967–8*

	UK[ab] 1968 (£m)	US[a] 1967 ($m)	Germany 1967 (DMm)
Gross output	5935	89979	69995
Purchase of raw materials, etc.	3238	49001	23646
Net output	2696	40978	46349
Employment (incl. working props.) (th)	1586·3	3605·1	2216·8

Sources: UK, *Census of Production 1968*; US, *Census of Construction 1967*; Germany, *Zensus im Produzierenden Gewerbe 1967*.
[a] Excluding self-employment activities.
[b] Includes opencast mining and construction plant hire.

respectively. In the United States and Germany opencast mining is classified as an extractive industry and hire of construction equipment as a service. To the extent that productivity in these two activities differs from British construction activity, the comparative productivity result will thus be impaired – but given their relatively small quantitative importance, to a minor extent only.[1]

A similar qualification will attach to the findings as a consequence of the inclusion of some self-employed construction activities in the German data, but their exclusion in the United Kingdom and United States. Since it is highly plausible that self-employed activities – performed with less capital and fewer ancillary services than other construction activities – will display a labour productivity level below average for the sector, the German results may be biased downwards on this account.

As stated, the methodology involves deflating the value added figures in table 11.1 to a common basis using price ratios provided by Kravis. The relevant ratios accord with our needs. They are based essentially on costings in the three countries of 'a representative sample of (building/construction) specifications for each detailed category'.[2]

Before these price indices can be applied to the output data in table 11.1, they need to be processed in two important respects. First, a series of weights – the values of construction output in the relevant categories for the specified years – are required to combine the component price ratios into an average for the construction industry as a whole. Obtaining these weights is not a straightforward procedure. This is partly due to the fact that censuses frequently do not break down construction output by type – educational buildings, roads, etc. In any

[1] The German data in table 1 have been adjusted to include constructional steelwork which, in Germany, is classified in manufacturing.
[2] Kravis *et al.*, 1975, p. 155.

Table 11.2. *Comparative productivity in construction, 1967–8*

	Standardised net output[a] (£ million)	Output per man (£)	Comparative productivity
UK, 1968	2696	1700	1·00
US, 1967	12232	3393	2·00
Germany, 1967	6546	2953	1·74

[a] At United Kingdom prices.

case censuses are not generally available for the years which are covered by Kravis price ratios. Fortunately in all three countries construction statistics from other sources are available by type of output and can be used as weights for combining the price ratios.

Secondly, the average price ratios so obtained need to be 'moved' from the Kravis years to the base years of table 11.1. The price ratios which emerge for 1967–8 are: US/UK 3·35 (with American quantity weights) and 3·55 (British quantity weights); Germany/UK 7·08 (German quantity weights) and 8·06 (Brtish quantity weights).

Using these price ratios in conjunction with the output and employment data of table 11.1 yields the comparative productivity results set out in table 11.2.[1] It is clear from the conceptual and practical measurement problems, and the methods adopted for their solution, that great reliability cannot be attached to these results. At best they must be regarded as probable orders of magnitude. The experience of Paige and Bombach was that 'the construction industry presented more serious difficulties than those encountered in any other sector'.[2] Whilst we were fortunate in having access to data – especially Kravis price indices – that were unavailable to these authors, it is clear that our measures of comparative productivity in this sector must be subject to a considerable margin of error.

DOUBLE DEFLATED RESULTS

The construction industry affords another opportunity to measure double deflated US/UK productivity using one of the methods applied to manufacturing.[3] It consists of combining the 1967–8 US/UK output price ratios obtained for manufacturing industries into a single US/UK

[1] An attempt was made to estimate sub-sector results in the case of the US/UK comparison, using basically the method outlined above. The result suggests that US/UK comparative productivity would appear to be smallest in the specialised trades, 1·81, and largest in civil engineering, 2·13, with general builders occupying an intermediate position, 1·92.

[2] *A Comparison of National Output*, p. 211.

[3] See chapter 10.

input price ratio for construction, using as weights the British construction industry's usage of raw materials from the various manufacturing sectors as shown in the 1968 British Input-Output tables. The procedure thus assumes that the pattern of raw material inputs into the construction industry in the United States is the same as the pattern of British inputs.

Since the input price ratio which emerges (3·10) is less than the gross output price ratio (3·55),[1] double deflation narrows the US/UK productivity differential, showing the British construction industry in a less unfavourable light. The differential, in United States prices, is reduced from 1·88 to 1·70.[2]

CONTEMPORARY PRODUCTIVITY

The procedure for deriving contemporary productivity comparisons from the results presented in table 11.2 is the standard one adopted in this project: for all three countries, base-year (1967 and 1968) standardised net outputs and employment are projected to current years by appropriate (real) output and employment indices, to yield contemporary measures of labour productivity on a comparative basis. The results for the construction industry are set out in table 11.3.

Table 11.3. *Comparative productivity in construction, 1968–77*

Year	Net output per man (£)[a]			Comparative productivity (UK = 1·00)	
	UK	US	Germany	US/UK	Germany/UK
1968	1700	3498	2916	2·06	1·72
1969	1759	3264	2998	1·86	1·70
1970	1889	3071	3223	1·63	1·71
1971	2031	3241	3312	1·59	1·63
1972	2009	3305	3312	1·65	1·65
1973	1937	3189	3299	1·65	1·70
1974	1802	2787	3275	1·55	1·82
1975	1716	2833	3304	1·65	1·93
1976	1603	2971	3595	1·85	2·24
1977	1737	2953	3795	1·70	2·18

Sources: table 11.2; UK, *Annual Abstract*; US, *Statistical Abstract* and *Monthly Labor Review*; Germany, *Statistisches Jahrbuch*.
[a] At 1968 prices.

[1] Because the input price ratio was obtained from UK weights, consistency requires that it be used, in the double deflation technique, with the UK quantity-weighted construction output price index.
[2] See table 3.3.

In the case of the United Kingdom, the output index which has been applied is the official one used as a component of the index of industrial production, in turn based on the value of new construction work (together with repairs and maintenance) at constant prices. Similarly, the United States output index is derived from changes, in constant prices, of the value of new construction. The index used for changes in German construction output is also an official one.[1]

It will be recalled that the basic productivity results for the United States and the United Kingdom were derived from output and labour force data that excluded the activities of the self-employed. In principle, the construction output indices referred to above embrace self-employed activities and therefore so should the labour force indices which are adopted. No such official series appear to be available for either the United States or for the United Kingdom. Accordingly, labour force indices derived from numbers of wage and salary employees have been used for all three countries. It should be appreciated that since these series exclude self-employed construction workers a potential error is introduced into the contemporary results for the industry.

Another qualification needs to be mentioned. The output of the industry accounts only for a part – though certainly the largest part – of total construction in the economy. The remainder, 'force account construction activity', consists of work performed by non-construction companies for themselves. The official construction output indices relate to *total* construction (at constant prices), not to output *per se* of the construction industry, whilst the labour force figures and temporal indices derived therefrom relate *only* to the industry.

RELIABILITY OF THE RESULTS

Productivity, and comparative productivity, in construction is more difficult to measure than in the case of any of the other industrial activities. This is especially unfortunate since it emerges that the results obtained for this sector are somewhat anomalous. In the US/UK comparison, the British construction sector emerges as (relatively) the best performer, in the Germany/UK comparison as the worst. There arises therefore a problem of interpretation, to determine whether the received picture reflects the real state of affairs, or whether it is no more than a statistical chimera. The resolution of the problem centres largely on the especially high German productivity which emerges.

The principal statistical problems encountered are: the difficulty of measuring, and comparing between countries, construction industry

[1] *Statistisches Jahrbuch.*

output; the comparative importance of self-employment in this activity; the behaviour of changes in recent years in American construction output, employment and productivity; and the unduly large ratio of net to gross output in the German industry.

There is little to say about the first of these problems, the method which we were obliged to use for standardising the sectors' outputs having been described above.[1] In the case of the second, any allowance for the numbers of self-employed in the United States and United Kingdom, and their inclusion in Germany, would tend to raise German productivity even more and thus contribute nothing to a statistical explanation of the paradox. Nor does an allowance for the third factor help. Even if American construction productivity is assumed to have increased over the period 1968 to 1977, by 20 per cent – rather than have declined, as it appears to have done, by 15 per cent – the US/UK ratio would still remain about the lowest among the sectors.

In the case of the fourth possibility, it must be recalled that if the German performance, and the Germany/UK ratio, were based on gross rather than net output, the Germany/UK differential would be (as with the US/UK differential) one of the lowest, not the highest. However, there is at present no statistical justification for preferring a gross output comparison to a net one. Indeed evidence from other sources suggests that, compared with other activities and other countries, value added per man in the German construction industry is indeed high. Taking GDP per man (in own currencies) as 100, in 1970, the contribution to GDP, per man, in the British construction industry was 88, in the United States it was 80, but in Germany it was 103.

Whilst the evidence suggests that the construction sector paradox ought not to be questioned on statistical grounds, there are good reasons, considered in chapters 4 and 5, why the results authentically reflect a true state of affairs and an especially good German performance in this activity.

[1] As an alternative to Kravis price ratios, the Germany/UK results were reworked using ratios of construction costs in the two countries from other sources. The productivity differential was not greatly changed.

12

PUBLIC UTILITIES

STRUCTURE OF THE INDUSTRY

This sector conveniently divides into four sub-sectors, gas, electricity, water and certain other activities. The latter category includes comparatively minor activities not found on any scale in the United Kingdom, steam supply and irrigation in the United States and district heating in Germany. Additionally, in the case of the United States, the 'other' activity category embraces some 'combination' companies, the gas and electricity activities of which cannot be separated. As table 12.1 shows

Table 12.1. *Public utilities basic data, 1975*

	Net output			Employment		
Industry[a]	UK (£m)	US[b] ($m)	Germany (DMm)	UK	US (thousands)	Germany
Gas	983	10200	1770	104·2	207·6	33·7
Electricity	1911	27900	25212	195·4	473·5	156·9
Water	442	..	1724	43·9	146·2	38·1
Other[c]	n.a.	..	141	n.a.	59·9	7·3
Public utilities	3336	..	28847	343·5	887·2	236·0

Sources: UK, *Census of Production, 1975*; US, American Gas Association, *Gas Facts Yearbook*, Edison Electric Institute, *Statistical Yearbook of the Electrical Utility Industry* and *Statistical Abstract*; Germany, *Statistisches Jahrbuch*.

[a] MLHs 601 (gas) and 602 (electricity) have been matched with US three digit classifications 491 and 492, respectively, and 493 (essentially 'combination companies') apportioned between them. MLH 603 has been identified with 494, and US 'other' comprises 496 and 497. In the case of the UK/Germany comparison, MLHs 601, 602 and 603 have been matched respectively with German classification numbers 10·3, 10·1 and 10·7.

[b] Estimated.

[c] Other activities in the US comprise mainly those of 'combination companies' that could not be allocated between gas and electricity, together with 'steam supply' and 'irrigation systems'. In Germany they comprise 'district heating'.

for 1975 – the most suitable common year for comparisons – the sector was dominated by the production and distribution of gas and electricity. Electricity production and supply bulks largest, accounting for more than half the sector's employment in all three countries, though its dominance is greatest in Germany.

As in the case of all sectors, overall comparative productivity ratios depend on the structure of the public utilities sector in each country. Also a special feature of the sector may do much to shape the productivity results which emerge: contrasts between the three countries in the precise nature of the activity which a given sub-sector embraces. Thus comparative productivity ratios for electricity will be influenced by the extent to which British electricity compared with German and American is derived from oil, coal or nuclear power stations. Such a qualification applies *a fortiori* to gas.

MEASURING COMPARATIVE PRODUCTIVITY

Gas

In the case of this sub-sector productivity will vary with the extent to which gas is derived from the processing of coal or oil and with the preponderance of natural gas in a country's output. For in all three countries, public utilities in effect buy natural gas from the extractive industries or from foreign suppliers, merely distributing the product. In the United Kingdom natural gas extraction activities extend from exploration and drilling etc. up to onshore pipelines to terminals and also to those terminals themselves. The activity measured here relates to the distribution of natural gas from these terminals to the consumer. In the United States the production and preparation of natural gas up to the point of shipment from the producing property is included in the extractive industries and its transmission and distribution thereafter in the public utilities.

Output measurement in the gas industry is simplified to the extent that the industry handles a product that is relatively homogenous and can be expressed in common physical units (therms). In practice the situation is complicated by the fact that there are certain ancillary 'outputs'. This complication is accommodated by the method described in chapter 2. Gas price ratios, of 1·57 and 6·75 for US/UK and Germany/UK respectively, are used to standardise American and German output values in £ sterling. In the case of the United States and United Kingdom these ratios are based on unit values obtained from physical gas output and corresponding sales values, in the case of Germany direct from price data.

Table 12.2 shows standardised output values, output per man and comparative productivity ratio for gas. The calculations on which the table is based reveal that in the case of both the Germany/UK and US/UK comparisons, there are substantial differences between the gross

Table 12.2. *Comparative productivity in public utilities, 1975*

	Output per man (£)			Comparative productivity UK = 1.00	
	UK	US	Germany	US/UK	Germany/UK
Gas	9433	31295	20840[a]	3.32	2.21
Electricity	9780	34661	20628	3.54	2.11
Water	10068	19829[b]	9963[b]	1.97	0.99
'Other'	n.a.	31265[b]	2616	n.a.	n.a.
Public utilities	9712	31200	18379	3.21	1.89

Sources: Table 12.1; see also text.
[a] Modified German data, see text.
[b] Estimated by reverse valuation technique.

and net productivity ratios which require further examination. German gas productivity is much better than British on a gross basis but somewhat worse when measured by net output per man, because of the large difference between the two industries in the ratio of net to gross output. In the United Kingdom, this ratio was 61 per cent in 1975, in Germany no more than 23 per cent. This in turn reflects the fact that the British industry obtained gas (from British North Sea fields) at a lower cost than Germany must pay for imported supplies from Russia, the Netherlands and Norway. On the other hand there is evidence that supplies to consumers are priced relatively highly in the United Kingdom compared with Germany.

The issue is very relevant to productivity measurement for it suggests that on this occasion, and somewhat exceptionally, greater weight should be attached to the gross comparative productivity ratio rather than to the net output ratio, since the latter may be distorted by national pricing policies. Accordingly, a series of modified German data have been inserted in table 12.2 for the gas industry (and for the total utilities sector).[1]

The discrepancy between gross and net productivity ratios is comparably large for the US/UK comparisons. In this case, as generally, there are reasons for placing most emphasis on the net productivity ratio. Gas supply in the United States is vertically disintegrated, so that compared with the United Kingdom where operations are conducted essentially by a single organisation gross output will be inflated by double counting when gas is sold from 'transmission' to 'distribution' establishments. Whilst reliance has been placed on net output concepts in the US/UK comparison, practical problems were posed by the

[1] These gas industry modifications are based on the reverse valuation technique.

absence of readily available net output values for the American gas industry, which therefore have been estimated.[1]

Electricity

Output and productivity measurement for the electricity industry is in principle comparatively easy since, again, the bulk of the sector's output comprises a single homogeneous product which in all three countries can be physically measured in a common unit, kilowatt hours. In each country the units of electrical output supplied by the industry are related to sales values yielding unit prices which, in turn, are converted into US/UK and Germany/UK price ratios of 1·70 and 7·79 respectively. These price ratios are used to standardise American and German gross and net output values, to a £ sterling basis, the sole practical difficulty in this procedure being the need to estimate – as in the case of the United States gas industry – net output in United States electricity.

Two other practical complications should be noted. First, output and productivity comparisons could be made only for part of the American electricity industry, the 'investor companies' which fortunately account for as much as 89 per cent of the whole industry's gross output and 87 per cent of its employment; the results obtained for this sub-sector have been extended to the whole industry. Secondly, in the United Kingdom and Germany, sales of the selected product, electricity, cover only a proportion of the industry's gross output, though the method is such that an allowance is made for this. The results are set out in table 12.2.

Water

In the United Kingdom, domestic water supply charges are usually based on a rating system, so that effectively the 'price' per unit of water varies from household to household. In these circumstances it was inappropriate to use our standard technique, deflating to a common currency output values for water supply in the three countries, using international water price ratios.

Instead, attention is directed from the outset at a physical relationship, the quantity of water supplied per employee, yielding a US/UK comparative productivity ratio of 1·97 and a Germany/UK ratio of 0·99. The valuation aspect cannot, of course, be entirely avoided: standardised net output per man is required for aggregating the productivity results with those obtained above for electricity and gas. The reverse valuation technique has been used for this purpose.

Water supply accounts for only a relatively small proportion of total public utility activity so that the precise method used for comparing

[1] Estimates were obtained by two methods which yielded reassuringly similar answers.

productivity in this sub-sector will have little impact on the overall result. This can be demonstrated by recalculating the Germany/UK productivity ratio for water supply using our standard approach based on international price indices. This method suggested comparative productivity ratios of 0·44 and 0·36 for gross and net output – very different from the sub-sector ratio of 0·99 obtained above. However, when these alternatives are embodied in the aggregation process, the total sector's Germany/UK productivity ratio is left comparatively undisturbed.

Other activities

Since this sub-sector is represented only in the United States and Germany, comparative productivity ratios, *vis-à-vis* the United Kingdom are inapplicable. Nevertheless, it is necessary to embrace these activities – district heating in Germany, steam supply, irrigation and some indivisible electricity/gas supplies in the United States – in the aggregation procedure. For Germany, gross and net output values for these activities are deflated to a standardised £ sterling basis by means of the overall Germany/UK price ratio implicit in the activities of the rest of the sector – gas, electricity and water. These ratios are 7·51 for gross output and 7·40 for net output. The same procedure cannot be adopted for the United States, where neither gross nor net output data are available for 'other activities'. Therefore it has been assumed that the overall US/UK productivity ratio for gas, electricity and water, applies also to 'other activities' and United States gross and net output for this sub-sector has been estimated by the reverse valuation technique.

Again the degree of error introduced into the overall sector result by these somewhat arbitrary procedures should not be unduly large. In neither the United States nor Germany does this sub-sector account for much of public utilities' activity.

CONTEMPORARY PRODUCTIVITY

Table 12.3 carries the comparative productivity results presented in table 12.2 to other years by means of appropriate output and employment data. For the United Kingdom, real output indices for the three sub-sectors, gas, electricity and water, were made available by the CSO and the 1975 census employment data were extended by means of the Department of Employment series of employees.

For Germany, official output indices are provided for the two principal sectors, gas and electricity, in the *Statistisches Jahrbuch*; employment indices for these two sectors were based on data presented in *Lange Reihen zur Wirtschaftsentwicklung*. Neither an output index nor comprehen-

Table 12.3. *Comparative productivity in public utilities, 1968–77*

UK = 1·00

	US/UK				Germany/UK			
Year	Gas	Electricity	Water	Public utilities	Gas	Electricity	Water	Public utilities
1968	7·36	4·06	1·77	4·26	1·56	1·93	0·82	1·74
1969	7·33	3·94	1·68	4·15	1·90	1·98	0·79	1·82
1970	7·05	3·71	1·66	3·97	2·18	1·96	0·78	1·84
1971	6·25	3·63	1·70	3·83	2·22	1·95	0·80	1·83
1972	4·92	3·45	1·60	3·45	2·03	1·88	0·78	1·72
1973	4·28	3·29	1·49	3·19	2·20	1·86	0·77	1·73
1974	3·72	3·38	1·70	3·16	2·19	2·02	0·84	1·81
1975	3·32	3·54	1·97	3·21	2·21	2·11	0·99	1·89
1976	3·21	3·56	2·07	3·22	2·23	2·25	1·09	2·02
1977	2·79	3·47	2·12	3·07	. .	. .	. .	1·89[a]

Sources: Table 12.2 and see text.
[a] Estimated.

sive employment data could be traced for the water sector. It proved necessary therefore to construct an output index for water from sales data contained in the *Jahresbericht* of the German Gas and Water Federation and it was assumed that in all years employment in this sector constituted, as in 1975, a fifth of the total gas and electricity labour force. It was also assumed that output and employment in 'other' activities in the German sector (accounting for not more than 3 per cent of employment in 1975) followed the combined output and employment changes of the German gas and electricity industries.

Real output series for gas, electricity and water in the United States were constructed from physical data relating to the output of these three activities. Output in the 'other' activity group (largely 'combination' companies which cannot be allocated between gas and electricity, accounting for less than 7 per cent of the sector's employment in 1975) was estimated, in each year, from per capita net output in the remainder of the sector (gas, electricity and water) together with the estimated employment level in 'other' activities. Employment series were estimated on the basis of Bureau of Labor Statistics and industry sources.

13

TRANSPORT AND COMMUNICATIONS

STRUCTURE OF THE INDUSTRY

This chapter is the longest, and most involved, of all the purely measurement sections of this study, in part reflecting the fact that no common method can be applied to productivity measurement for its many constituent parts. As a first step the component industries of the sector are matched and the structure of the transport sector in the three countries compared in table 13.1 on the basis of employment data.

Table 13.1. *Employment structure of transport and communications, 1970–2*

	UK 1972		US 1972		Germany 1970	
	(th)	(%)	(th)	(%)	(th)	(%)
Transport						
Railways	243	16	575	13	414	28
Road passenger	228	15	365	8	130	9
Road haulage	246	16	1126	26	179	12
Sea transport, ports and inland waterways	179	12	218	5	92	6
Air transport	77	5	363	8	26	2
Miscellaneous	128	8	133	3	168	11
Posts and telecommunications	442	29	1612	37	457	31
Transport and communications	1543	100	4392	100	1466	100

Sources: UK, *Annual Abstract*; US, Interstate Commerce Commission, *Transport Statistics in the United States*, Bureau of the Census, *Census of Public Employment, Statistical Abstract*; Germany, *Unternehmen und Arbeitsstätten Heft 3*.

Value added by the individual transport industries would be preferable, but these data are difficult to obtain for all three countries on a comparable basis. Whilst official labour force statistics are more easily come by for these activities, they are by no means those which ideally are required and, for example, exclude self-employed.[1]

[1] Whilst exclusion of the self-employed can be of no great overall significance in this sector, it clearly is important in certain activities. Among these are road haulage and, more especially, taxi services. Indeed, lack of labour force data for the latter activity (classified to road passenger transport) has precluded a specific productivity comparison; later the activity's equivalent output has been deducted from passenger transport contribution to GDP.

The British and American data in table 13.1 relate to 1972. Most of the UK/US transport productivity measurement and comparison are made for that year when in a number of activities American census results were uniquely available. The German employment data relate to 1970. The table enables us to comment on the sizes, in employment terms, of the various sub-sectors. First, the apparent similarity in the relative importance of British and American rail traffic is misleading. In the United Kingdom 65 per cent of rail receipts in 1972 were from passenger traffic; in the United States this source constituted a mere 3 per cent. In Germany too, railways are much more concerned with freight than passenger movement, and this, together with a relatively smaller road haulage activity, helps to account for the large numbers employed on German railways.

When the scale of implied freight movement by rail in the United States is added to the much higher American share of road haulage it appears that there is a disproportionately large amount of freight movement in the United States compared with the United Kingdom. However, it is difficult to be sure about this for it should be appreciated that much own-account freight transportation by companies is included in the activity of the manufacturing sector.

A relatively large role for road passenger transport in the United Kingdom reflects both more widespread use of cars and air transport in America, and of cars in Germany. That in all three countries the significance of air transport seems comparatively low is also due to a statistical chimera, the use of employment rather than (value added) output data.

Finally, sea transport (including ports and inland waterways) account for 12 per cent of the sector's employment in the United Kingdom but no more than 5 and 6 per cent respectively in the United States and Germany – reflecting both the greater significance of international trade in the British economy and of the merchant navy in its sectoral activities. The relative importance of posts and telecommunications activities appears to differ little between the three countries, accounting for 29, 31 and 37 per cent of the labour force, respectively in the United Kingdom, Germany and the United States.

The productivity comparisons which follow do not necessarily relate to the totality of a sub-sector as measured in table 13.1 so that there are some discrepancies between the employment data in this and later tables. Instead, wherever possible, an attempt has been made to take basic data from sources that are internally consistent in the sense that they contain both the output and labour force data from which the productivity measures are derived. In most cases these samples of each transport sub-sector cover the bulk of the activity in question. The

US/UK comparisons have been made for 1972, the most recent year for which detailed American census data were available. In the case of Germany/UK comparisons the data are such that sub-sector comparisons are best made for 1970.

MEASURING PRODUCTIVITY IN TRANSPORT AND COMMUNICATIONS

The activities embraced by this sector may seem quite disparate. In fact remarkably common themes characterise the productivity measurement issues which are encountered in the various activities – even those as different as transport and communications. It is the purpose of this section to identify these common themes and to narrow down the labour productivity measures which are in principle appropriate.

A labour productivity measure based on vehicle miles (bus, train, plane, ship etc.) per man would hardly be satisfactory in the present context. Passengers or tons carried per man are also conceptually unsuitable. In failing to take account of distance travelled, such a measure would introduce serious biases in American–British comparisons. Average length of journey for the United States road haulage industry is 306 miles compared with a mere 38 in the United Kingdom and failure to take some account of this would grossly understate American output and productivity. Clearly some account needs to be taken of distance as well as number of units transported. Passenger-miles or ton-miles per man approaches this requirement and is a superior productivity measure, according with a concept of (transport) output provided for and used by the economy, that is realised output per man.

Whilst this concept is a much more acceptable labour productivity measure, in most circumstances, crudely applied, it would still yield a biased picture of inter-country productivity differentials. Transporting a load over a given distance comprises not only a pure carriage element – for instance involving a lorry, a driver, and a given amount of time – but also a certain amount of loading and unloading work, a 'terminal work element'. It is largely irrelevant for our productivity measure whether or not the driver in question is himself responsible for this work. The turn-round time – perhaps waiting whilst the terminal work is undertaken – means that, *ceteris paribus*, two ten ton journeys of fifty miles involve more work and time than one ten ton journey of a hundred miles. Thus an unadjusted, ton-miles per man, productivity comparison, based on the average American and British road hauls of 306 and 38 miles, would be significantly biased in favour of the United States. The terminal element is an important constituent of the whole transport service which the consumer receives and, as such, should be reflected, along with distance and quantity, in output and labour productivity.[1]

This terminal element is present in virtually all transport activities – railways, road passenger, road haulage, maritime and air transport. It is also a feature of postal services, the collection and delivery of mail (highly labour intensive) as opposed to its long distance carriage, and of telecommunications too – the maintenance of the system as opposed to actual phone calls.

The need for, and ability to, adjust productivity measures for this terminal work factor varies between different transportation activities. In some activities a rough separation of 'terminal' and pure transportation activities, together with their respective labour forces, is possible. This is the case in sea transport, where port activities can be separated from sea going work and in air transport where terminal activities – air control, loading, unloading etc. – can to some extent be set apart from flying. This procedure is moreover especially important in these two activities where much terminal work – ports and airports – is provided for ships and aircraft other than those operated by the domestic maritime and airline carriers.

Another possibility is that the terminal element can be ignored in the inter-country productivity comparisons either because it is relatively insignificant or because it exerts a fairly uniform effect due to the fact that the average distance involved is approximately the same in the countries in question. This assumption, which has been made in the case of local passenger transport, usually has greater validity for UK/Germany comparisons than for UK/US comparisons.

Thirdly, and more generally, passenger-miles or ton-miles might be weighted with factors that reflect the total output package – terminal and carriage – associated with various distances. Such weights, normally prices or operating costs quoted for various specified distances, differ relatively as well as absolutely between countries, but are frequently only available for one. When there are available traffic movements classified by distances for each of which a 'price' is available then, effectively, this approach to productivity measurement reduces to the general one outlined in chapter 2. The various journey distances and their prices (or average values) can be used to derive an international price-ratio[2] for the sector in the two countries. Such a ratio is especially useful when, as in postal services, non-postal work (social benefit payments, banking services etc.) constitutes a significant proportion of output. For the price ratio, derived from essentially comparable activi-

[1] Frequency of stops in some forms of transport is indeed a major element in the service.

[2] Or two price ratios if weights and prices are available for the specified distances in both countries.

ties, can be used to deflate and standardise the output value of the complete activity.

A separate, though related, adjustment is that necessitated by international contrasts in the commodity mix which characterise a given transport activity. The nature of the loads carried by a given form of transportation can be very different, at the extreme both passengers and freight, on railways, ships and planes. But there is also enormous variety within freight, from bulk movements of ores, oils and grains etc. to small parcels of highly valuable items. Where necessary and possible, transportation of such disparate units has been aggregated into a single output figure using prices, or unit transport charges, as weights, the approach described in chapter 2.

In all three countries transport services are subsidised to varying degrees. This complicates the productivity comparisons at both the conceptual and practical levels. On the conceptual side, relative market prices may be distorted by subsidies as reflections of the inherent factor costs of different transport services. On the practical side – in the cases where this method is adopted – it is important that price ratios used to deflate output values to a standardised (£ sterling) basis be consistent with the output values to which they are applied. This latter requirement is frequently complicated by uncertainty as to the precise extent to which American and German output values include subsidy elements. The valuation problem is avoided – or effectively postponed to the aggregation section – in those instances where, initially, the productivity comparison is based on purely physical units.

SUB-SECTORAL PRODUCTIVITY COMPARISONS

Railways

American railways carry almost wholly freight traffic, British railways both freight and passengers. The productivity measurement methodology takes account of this contrast, though no further adjustment (for differences in the commodity mix in type of freight for example) was possible. In accordance with the basic approach employed in this study, the various component outputs – in this case passengers and freight – have been summed in the two countries, using value weights. After considerable experimentation it was decided to employ, in this instance, British weights only. In large part, this is due to the fact that the activity is substantially subsidised, and there is uncertainty about the extent to which subsidies are included in American (and German) output valuations.

On the passenger side, output in both countries is measured by passenger miles, no adjustment being made for inter-country differences

Table 13.2. *Comparative railway productivity*

	Standardised output value (£m)	Employment (th)	Output per man (£)	Comparative productivity
US/UK 1970				
United Kingdom	632[a]	199	3176	1·00
United States	6609	527	12541	3·95
Germany/UK 1970				
United Kingdom	559	208	2688	1·00
Germany	1166	401	2908	1·08

Sources: UK, *British Rail, Annual Accounts*; US, *Statistical Abstract*; Germany, *Statistisches Jahrbuch.*

[a] This includes, in addition to passengers and freight output, significant receipts for transportation of parcels, an item which in the US is moved principally by road and air.

in the terminal work element since the average distances travelled (23 miles in the United Kingdom and 33 in the United States) are fairly similar. The weight applied to this output is average revenue per passenger mile in the United Kingdom. Use of this weight simultaneously enables passenger output to be added to freight output and expresses American output in a standardised, £ sterling, figure. The weight has been adjusted to include subsidies for 'passenger support' in an attempt to make it reflect as much as possible the factor cost of providing passenger, relative to freight, services.

The average American freight haul, 306 miles, was about four times longer than the British, 76 miles, so that it proved necessary to make an adjustment for the terminal work element. This was achieved by taking, in both countries, two indicators of freight output, tons carried for terminal work and ton-miles for the transportation element. These two elements have been aggregated by means of estimates of British handling costs per ton and transport costs per ton-mile.

When these outputs are summed and British railways credited with the carriage of a significant quantity of parcels, table 13.2 yields a comparative US/UK productivity ratio of about four. With such a sharp contrast in the output composition of the two rail systems, the result is sensitive to the passenger/freight weighting system. With American weights, which very likely would attach higher relative values to passenger movements and lower ones to freight, the comparison would almost certainly emerge more favourably for the United Kingdom. However, some experimentation (based on estimates of American rail receipts from passenger and freight traffic) suggests that the ratio would probably not be reduced below 3½.

The German rail system is more akin to the British than the

American, since it handles significant quantities of both passengers and freight. The methodology applied in the US/UK comparison, the summation of passengers and freight outputs using British value weights, is used, though in the case of the Germany/UK freight comparison the need for a separation of the terminal work element is obviated by the absence of undue differences in length of haul. These results are also presented in table 13.2.

Local and road passenger transport

In the US/UK comparison it proved impracticable to embrace two significant activities in this sub-sector, taxi services and long distance bus services. Lack of data precluded the former and 'matching' problems the latter. As a result, the employment coverage shown for both the United Kingdom and United States in table 13.3 is significantly less than shown in table 13.1. The implicit assumption is that the comparative productivity ratio measured for the covered activities is applicable to the non-covered areas. A test, albeit a rough one, suggests that inclusion of estimates for long distance bus services would make little material difference to the result.

Table 13.3. *Comparative productivity in local and road passenger transport*

	Weighted passenger journeys (million equivalent)	Employment (th)	Output per man (th)	Comparative productivity 1970	Comparative productivity 1972[a]
US/UK 1970					
United Kingdom	4418	134[b]	33·0	1·00	1·00
United States	6600	138[b]	47·8	1·45	1·34
Germany/UK 1970					
United Kingdom	9826	265	37·1	1·00	
Germany	6170	124	49·8	1·34	

Sources: UK, Department of the Environment, *Transport Statistics*; US, *Statistical Abstract*; Germany, *Statistisches Jahrbuch*.

[a] Derived by adjusting 1970 results on the basis of changes in passenger journeys and in employment.

[b] Excludes employment on long distance buses.

The activities eventually covered by the comparison comprise British 'stage' bus services and American 'mass transit' bus services, together with the underground activities of the London Transport Executive and American mass transit railways. Mass transit workers in the United States cannot be allocated between road and railway activities so that there is a need to make a single productivity comparison, aggregating the outputs of local road and rail activities. This aggregation has been based on British weights, derived from value added per passenger carried on stage bus services and the underground.

Almost by definition the distances involved in mass transit systems, bus and rail, should be similar even in countries otherwise as different as the United States and the United Kingdom. This is fortuitous not merely in terms of avoiding adjustments for terminal work elements, but also because data pertaining to average journey lengths are difficult to come by in the case of short passenger hauls. In any event the relative dominance of terminal work – stopping and starting, loading and unloading – in short haul passenger services means that numbers of passenger journeys is conceptually almost as suitable as passenger miles.

In the case of the Germany/UK comparison it is possible to embrace long distance bus (but not taxi) services. Because of the nature of the German data it proved necessary to aggregate the outputs of the various sub-sectors measured in passenger journeys. Again (for reasons given above) in the case of local transport, both bus and rail systems, little is likely to be lost by using passenger journeys rather than passenger miles. Likewise for long distance bus services, the use of passenger journeys should introduce little error since average journey lengths in the United Kingdom and Germany probably do not differ greatly. The comparison is in any event dominated by short hauls.

Road Haulage

This sector aptly illustrates the issues raised in the methodological section. On the basis of a crude comparison of ton-miles per employee, American labour productivity would seem to be much greater than British. However, the comparatively large element of terminal work associated with a British average haul of 38 miles compared with 306 miles in the United States means that such a measure exaggerates American output and productivity. Therefore the figures of ton-miles in the two countries have been adjusted in table 13.4 by the relative costs of operating short and long distance haulage. These relative costs per mile were derived from British vehicle operating costs.

It can be seen from table 13.4 that this procedure yields for 1972 a comparative US/UK productivity ratio of 1·80.[1] Effectively, the above comparison is between the whole of the British road haulage industry and the larger (class 1 motor carriers) American operators. Should productivity differ significantly between large and small operators then, of course, bias would be present in this ratio.

[1] An alternative method applied to 1966 data suggested a comparative US/UK ratio of 1·68, which when brought forward produced a ratio of 1·72 for 1972.

Table 13.4. *Comparative road haulage productivity*

US/UK 1972	UK	US
Ton-miles per employee (th)	137	329
Standardised cost per vehicle mile (pence)	24·4	18·3
Adjusted ton-miles per employee (th)	183	329
Comparative productivity	1·00	1·80
Germany/UK 1970	**UK**	**Germany**
Tonne-km transported (m)	51017	45900
Average length of haul (km)	65·8	57·1
Employment (th)	235·3	166·6
Tonne-km per employee (th)	216·8	275·5
Comparative productivity	1·00	1·27

Sources: UK, *Transport Statistics*; US Interstate Commerce Commission, *Transport Statistics in the United States*; United Nations, *Annual Bulletin of Transport Statistics for Europe*; Germany, *Statistisches Bundesamt Unternehmen und Arbeitsstätten.*

In view of the similarity in average length of haul no adjustments need be made for the terminal work element in the Germany/UK comparison. Table 13.4 suggests that, in 1970, tonne-kilometres per man in Germany were some 1·27 times greater than in the United Kingdom. No quantitative allowance for contrasts in the commodity mix moved by the two sectors appears practicable.

Sea transport, ports and inland waterways

It is essential to sub-divide this activity into at least two sub-sectors, water transport and port activities. In the former, productivity measurement relates labour force to goods and passengers transported by domestic carriers, in the latter, the 'output' is goods and passengers of all carriers, domestic or otherwise, handled in the ports. Though necessitated by the distinction in output coverage, this sub-division confers a significant advantage on the productivity measures. In effect, it separates much – though not all – of the terminal work element from transportation activities *per se*.

In the shipping sub-sector contrasts between the United Kingdom and the United States are most in evidence, especially the predominance of international services in the British sector and the importance of internal water transportation – Great Lakes, rivers and canals – in the American.[1] The British fleet is larger and consists of proportionately more tankers, ore and bulk carriers, but fewer general cargo boats.

[1] In both countries very short distance inland traffic has been bracketed with port activities largely because of the common usage of tugboat and towing services.

Table 13.5. *Comparative productivity in shipping*

US/UK 1972	UK	US
Tons of freight (m)	129·7	824·7
Average haul (miles)	3315	809
Ton-miles (billion)	430·0	667·2
Employment (th)	80·0[a]	73·1
Ton-miles per man (th)	5375	9127
Comparative productivity	1·00	1·70
Germany/UK 1970	**UK**	**Germany**
Tonnes of freight (m)	119·2	174·9
Employment (th)	81·1	62·7
Tonnes per man	1469	2790
Comparative productivity	1·00	1·90

Sources: UK, *Transport Statistics, Annual Abstract*; US, *Statistical Abstract*; Germany, *Statistisches Jahrbuch.*

[a] Excludes Sealink ferry-service employment.

Productivity calculations for shipping services must allow for differences in length of haul and in commodity composition. Because of a preponderance of internal water transport in the United States, and of international services in the activities of the British sector, differences in hauls are large. The average haul of the British shipping sector, 3315 miles, is four times greater than that of the United States, 809 miles. Accordingly, the US/UK productivity comparison in table 13.5 is based on ton-miles. In the case of this sector some adjustment is automatically made for the proportionately greater terminal work element associated with the shorter journeys by the separate consideration of transportation and of port activities. However, no allowance is possible for variations in time spent waiting at ports. Inter-country differences in this factor therefore contribute to the comparative productivity ratios which emerge.

A fairly crude allowance has been made for differences in the freight/passenger pattern. Whereas total passenger movements through British and American ports are known, the number of passengers carried by the respective domestic carriers is not. That British ports handle seven times more passengers than American is largely due to the importance of ferry services to the Continent and Ireland. Accordingly the data in table 13.5 have been roughly adjusted for this difference by excluding from the British labour force the 6000 seagoing employees of the British Rail ferry service and major British ferry operators. Ideally, the long distance passengers carried by British and American ships should still be taken into account on the output side of the equation.

Table 13.6. *Comparative port productivity*

US/UK 1972	UK	US
Tons of freight (th)	346347	1441071
Numbers of passengers (th)	11999	1751
Total equivalent tons (th)	374404	1445168
Employment (th)	90	140
Equivalent tons per employee	4160	10323
Comparative productivity	1·00	2·48
Germany/UK 1970	**UK**	**Germany**
Tonnes of freight (th)	352175	141157
Employment (th)	101·1	20·8
Tonnes per man	3483	6786
Comparative productivity	1·00	1·95

Sources: UK, *Transport Statistics, Annual Abstract*; US, *Statistical Abstract*; Germany, *Statistisches Jahrbuch.*

Data limitations prevent this, but such activity is now minimal in relation to the freight flows.

Whilst it proved impossible to separate port operations from short-haul inland waterways activities (the latter activity accounts for only 17 per cent of the sub-sector's labour force in the United States, and for a mere 2 per cent in the United Kingdom), output measurement is restricted to quantity of freight and numbers of passengers handled by the ports. Freight and passengers have been aggregated on the basis of British 'dues' per ton and per passenger. Even in the United Kingdom, where passenger handling is relatively more important, it constitutes, on this weighted basis, no more than $7\frac{1}{2}$ per cent of port activity. It has not been possible to make any allowance for different kinds of cargo, 'restow' movements or transhipment traffic. Table 13.6 suggests a comparative US/UK port productivity ratio of 2·48. Since a somewhat higher proportion of this sub-sector's labour force in the United States is occupied on short-haul inland waterways the result perhaps understates the true difference.

There would be difficulty in separating German waterway activity – much more important than in the United Kingdom – from sea and coastal shipping. However, since the average haul on German inland waterways is 200 km compared with 20 km for British inland waterways, it is more akin to British coastal traffic which is characterised by an average haul of 450 km. For this reason a single productivity ratio covering sea, coastal shipping and inland waterways has been derived. Again the calculations ignore passenger traffic which now contributes only a minimal amount to the receipts of this sector. Unfortunately, the output of the sector could be measured only by weight of freight moved, not by ton miles, due to the inadequacy of German information about lengths of haul. Since the average British haul is probably significantly longer than the German, the productivity ratio for this sub-sector, given in table 13·5, will be biased somewhat in Germany's favour.

Productivity levels in the port activities of the two countries have been measured by weight of freight handled per man, and the results are presented in table 13.6.

Air transport

The air transport sub-sector is divided into two activities, air services, external and domestic, provided by the country's airlines and airport services – baggage handling, flight control, etc. – provided both for domestic and foreign airlines. This separation posed problems of some complexity, but is necessary not only on account of inherent differences in the scope and nature of the two activities, but also because productivity levels and differentials in airport activities could differ markedly from those of airline activities. Assumptions that need to be made when measuring airport productivity are such that the reliability of the results is inferior to those obtained for airline activity. Fortunately, airport activity is a comparatively minor constituent of total air transport output. Revenue of the British Airports Authority was less than a tenth of total British airline receipts in 1972.[1]

Adding the two physical units of airline 'output', quantity of freight and number of passengers, is relatively straightforward. Because weight is the critical factor in air transport both are measured and summed in official sources in terms of ton-miles. In any event the output 'mix' between freight and passengers is very similar in all three countries. No adjustment is made for terminal work elements. Lengths of haul are similar and/or comparatively long, so that any such adjustment would have only a minimal impact.[2] Also any differences in terminal work elements are largely accommodated by the separation of airline and airport activities. The results are presented for the UK/US and UK/Germany comparisons (1972 and 1970 respectively) in table 13.7.

There are three principal indicators of work done at airports – airliner movements, numbers of passengers and tons of freight handled. Whilst

[1] Airport activity is of similar comparative importance in Germany and rather less so in the United States.

[2] This assumption was tested by standardising for differences in lengths of haul on scheduled passenger travel in the United States and United Kingdom. The method was based on the average cost and revenue per passenger mile over different lengths of haul in the United States. A comparison of the distribution of lengths of haul between the United States and United Kingdom on the basis of these costs suggested that the British ton-mile measure of work done would be increased by a factor of less than 1 per cent.

Table 13.7. *Comparative airline productivity*

US/UK 1972	UK	US
Total ton-miles all services (m)	2573·9	21666·8
Employment (th)	55·4[a]	307·0
Ton-miles per man	46460	70576
Comparative productivity	1·00	1·52
Germany/UK 1970	**UK**	**Germany**
Total tonne-km all services (m)	3442·8	1949
Employment (th)	51·1[a]	18·2
Tonne-km per man	67374	107088
Comparative productivity	1·00	1·59

Sources: UK, Civil Aviation Authority, *Annual and Monthly Statistics* and *Transport Statistics*; US, Civil Aeronautics Board, *Handbook of Airline Statistics* and *Statistical Abstract*; International Civil Aviation Organisation (ICAO), *Digest of Statistics*; Germany, *Statistisches Jahrbuch.*

[a] The division of UK employment between airlines and airports is estimated on the basis of information given in the *Annual Accounts* of the British Airports Authority.

Table 13.8. *Comparative airport productivity*

US/UK[a] 1972	UK	US	Comparative productivity ratio (UK = 1·00)
Passengers at major airports (th)	28574	135948	
Freight and mail at major airports (tons)	565855	3685352	
Employment (th)	20·6	43·3	
Passengers per employee	1387	3140	2·26
Freight and mail, tons per employee	27·5	85·1	3·10
Average comparative productivity ratio			2·68
Germany/UK 1970	**UK**	**Germany**	**Comparative productivity ratio (UK = 1·00)**
Passengers handled (th)	32400	15400	
Freight and mail (tonnes)	628722	288257	
Employment (th)	19·2	8·2	
Passengers per employee	1688	1878	1·11
Freight and mail tonnes per employee	32·7	35·2	1·07
Average comparative productivity ratio			1·09

Sources: See table 13.7.

[a] Data are available for the 'output' of major airports only in the US, these are compared with major UK airports (those operated by BAA) but in both countries employment totals are for the whole activity.

the latter two are used here as indicators of output no satisfactory means of aggregating them was found. Fortunately the ratio of passengers to tons of freight is not hugely different in the three countries, so that either, divided by ratios of airport employment, yield productivity ratios that are not too dissimilar, especially in the Germany/UK comparison. Arithmetic averages of the two component ratios have therefore been used in table 13.8 to measure comparative productivity for airport activity. Airport services are a small fraction of total air transport activity and any errors in the productivity comparisons for this sub-sector will have only a small impact on productivity differentials for the sector as a whole.

Obtaining suitable weights for combining productivity in airlines and airports poses some problems. In all three countries the gross output of airlines – total receipts – is available, but involves an element of double counting in that airport landing charges, both for domestic and overseas operations, are effectively included. In the end, the relationship between the British Airports Authority revenue and total British airline revenue of 7 per cent in 1970 and 8 per cent in 1972 has been used. Using the reverse valuation technique,[1] these weights yield for the US/UK comparison a ratio for total air transport activity of 1·78 and for the Germany/UK comparison a productivity differential of 1·50.

Posts and telecommunications

In all three countries this sub-sector embraces a wide range of peripheral activities such as the provision of certain banking services, the payment of some social security benefits and data processing. But the two principal activities which account for the bulk of the sub-sector's output, and on which the productivity comparisons are founded, are postal services and the operation of the telephone system.

In the context of productivity comparisons, the dominant characteristic of postal services is the preponderance of a terminal work element comprising sorting, delivery, counter and other handling services. In both the United Kingdom and United States pure carriage costs are less than ten per cent of the total so that the greater postal area of the United States can effectively be ignored, and attention directed to pieces handled rather than ton-miles.

A necessary assumption in the comparison is that the 'commodity mix', the composition of the mail carried, is broadly the same and in both countries parcels constitute only a very small proportion of the number of items carried. The number of physical units handled, in conjunction with postal income, yields an average cost per piece in each

[1] See chapter 2 and Technical Note.

Table 13.9. *Comparative productivity in postal services, US/UK, 1972*

	UK		US
Total income (m)	£603·8[a]		$9840·3
Postal income (m)	£489·4[a]		$8399·0
Total pieces handled (m)	10984		89683
Average value per piece (pence and cents)	4·46		9·37
Price ratio		2·10	
Standardised output (£m)	£603·8		£4685·9
Employment (th)	184[b]		625
Output per man (£)	3282		7497
Comparative productivity	1·00		2·28

Sources: UK, Post Office, *Annual Report and Accounts*; US, *Statistical Abstract.*

[a] Factor cost, i.e. including subsidies.
[b] Including an allocation of staff at headquarters.

country and, in turn, as US/UK price ratio.[1] This ratio is used to deflate total income of the sub-sector to a standardised sterling value and thus output per man. In both countries somewhat exceptionally in this study – part-time workers have been counted as equivalent to one half a full-time worker in table 13.9.

Output measurement in telecommunications services is not straightforward. Not only must the number of phone calls be counted as output but also work involved in the maintenance of the system. In brief this is achieved by converting the size of the system, measured by number of telephones, into an equivalent number of phone calls. This is done by employing, as weights, average rental per telephone divided by the average cost of a phone call, weights which differ significantly between the American and British systems. Relating the number of phone calls (actual plus equivalent) to telephone revenue, yields an implied cost per call in each of the countries, from which price ratios are derived. These are employed to standardise the total telecommunications revenue from which comparative US/UK productivity is obtained in table 13.10.

Uncertainty about the proper apportionment of the total German labour force between the postal and telecommunication services requires that the Germany/UK productivity comparison be made for the two services jointly. Again attention focuses on the derivation of the price ratio, in this case used for standardising total revenue from posts and telecommunications. It is a weighted average of two UK/Germany price

[1] This was preferred to a directly observed purchasing power parity since there are no clear identities between American 1st, 2nd, 3rd and 4th class mail, and British 1st and 2nd class. Additionally the way in which scales of charges vary with weight differs in the two countries.

Table 13.10. *Comparative productivity in telecommunications, US/UK, 1972*

	UK		US
Total revenue (m)	£884·1		$23429
Telephone revenue (m)	£785·0		$22769
Equivalent numbers of phone calls: UK weights (m)	21298		260737
Equivalent number of phone calls: US weights (m)	53612		473713
Price ratio: UK weights		2·37	
Price ratio: US weights		3·29	
Standardised output: EK weights (£m)	884·1		9885·7
Standardised output: US weights (£m)	884·1		7121·3
Employment (th)	241		849
Output per man: UK weights (£)	3668		11644
Output per man: US weights (£)	3668		8388
Comparative productivity: UK weights	1·00		3·17
Comparative productivity: US weights	1·00		2·29

Sources: UK, Post Office, *Annual Report and Accounts*; US, *Statistical Abstract*.

ratios, relating respectively to the postal and telephone services. The weights used are the respective British and German revenues from these two services. As in the case of the UK/US comparison the postal price ratio is derived from the average value per piece handled in the two countries and the phone price ratio is derived from telephone receipts and numbers of equivalent calls. In this case however it was practical to use only British rentals and call charges for obtaining the equivalent call weights. The resulting price ratios, 11·81 on British weights and 11·67 on German weights, are employed to derive the standardised outputs of table 13·11.

Table 13.11. *Comparative productivity in posts and telecommunications, Germany/UK, 1970*

	UK		Germany
Total revenue (m)	£1135·4		DM 15110
Price ratios (Germany/UK): UK weights		11·81	
Price ratios (Germany/UK): GR weights		11.67	
Standardised output (£m): UK weights	1135·4		1279·4
Standardised output (£m): GR weights			1294·8
Employment (th)	426·1[a]		451·1
Output per man (£): UK weights	2665		2836
Output per man (£): GR weights			2870
Comparative productivity: UK weights	1·0		1·06
Comparative productivity: GR weights			1·08

Sources: UK, Post Office, *Annual Report and Accounts*; Germany, *Statistisches Jahrbuch*.

[a] UK total employment has been adjusted to include sub-postmasters working on a part-time basis.

AGGREGATION OF SUB-SECTOR RATIOS

The reverse valuation technique[1] – employing British sub-sectoral net outputs – has been used to aggregate the comparative productivity ratios obtained above for the constituent activities of the transport and communications sector. The requirements of this technique pose a practical problem because the sources which we were obliged to use for productivity measures in this sector yielded, at best, only gross outputs (total receipts) but not net outputs for the component activities. In consequence, it was necessary to estimate the requisite British net outputs. It is possible, by interpolation, to estimate value added for the various British sub-sectors in 1972 using the 1970 and 1975 'weights' from which official estimates of changes in GDP at constant factor cost are derived.[2] These interpolated weights are in turn used to allocate United Kingdom GDP in 1972 between the component transport activities. The outcome of the aggregation procedure is a comparative US/UK 1972 productivity ratio of 2·16 for transport, 3·02 for telecommunications and 2·50 for the whole sector.

The same technique is used to derive an overall ratio from the results obtained for the sub-sectors in the 1970 Germany/UK comparison. In this case British net outputs, derived directly from the CSO 1970 'weights', yield a Germany/UK productivity ratio of 1·27 for transport, 1·08 for telecommunications and 1·21 for the whole sector.

CONTEMPORARY PRODUCTIVITY

Real output indices for the component activities of the sector were not readily available for the United States and Germany. It was only possible therefore to extend the base year results to other years for the sector as a whole, and in the case of the US/UK comparisons for the two principal sub-divisions, transport and communications. Output series used in each country for this purpose were largely based on the sector's contribution to GDP at constant prices. Employment series are taken from the *Annual Abstract* for the United Kingdom, the *Statistical Abstract* for the United States and the *Statistisches Jahrbuch* for Germany. Results are presented in table 13.12.

[1] See chapter 2 and Technical Note.

[2] See CSO, 'The Measurement of Changes in Production', *Studies in Official Statistics No. 25*, 1976 Appendix III and *National Income and Expenditure*.

Table 13.12. *Comparative productivity in transport and communications, 1968–77*

UK = 1·00

Year	US/UK comparison			Germany/UK comparison
	Transport	Communications	Transport and communications	
1968	2·40	2·84	2·62	1·15
1969	2·31	2·80	2·54	1·18
1970	2·22	2·91	2·51	1·21
1971	2·14	3·02	2·49	1·17
1972	2·16	3·02	2·50	1·10
1973	2·09	2·97	2·43	1·02
1974	2·04	2·95	2·40	1·05
1975	2·04	3·23	2·52	1·06
1976	2·12	3·37	2·63	1·08
1977	2·13	3·34	2·64	1·14

14

TECHNICAL NOTE

Gross output productivity comparisons

The principal method used in this report for making international output comparisons consists of weighting the physical units of the component elements of an industry's output in two countries by a common set of price weights. If relative prices in the United Kingdom are used as weights then an output comparison (which in turn may be related to a labour force comparison) can be made, for a given activity, between the United Kingdom and the United States in the form:

$$\frac{\Sigma pkqs}{\Sigma pkqk}$$

where: p denotes price of each component output
q denotes quantity of each component output
k denotes United Kingdom
s denotes United States.

If relative US prices are used, the output comparisons emerge as:

$$\frac{\Sigma psqs}{\Sigma psqk}$$

The extent of the divergence between these two measures of relative output will depend on the degree of difference between the two countries in the industry's output and price patterns. Usually, a country's comparative productivity performance is superior when outputs are aggregated on the basis of the other country's weights: domestic quantities tend to be relatively large when domestic prices are relatively low and vice versa. Normally, however, the disparity is not unduly large. It was found that on the basis of a 1967–8 comparison of the manufacturing sector, comparative US/UK productivity (UK = 1·00) was 2·76 using British weights and 2·52 using American weights.

Occasionally, sharp contrasts in output and price patterns yield much larger differences. In the late sixties coffee bulked large in the output of the American miscellaneous food industry, accounting for some 36 per cent of sales, in Britain 14 per cent. In contrast tea's share of American sales was 5 per cent, but of British, 36 per cent. In conjunction with very disparate price ratios (US$ per UK£), 1·50 for coffee and 6·76 for tea, very different comparative US/UK productivity ratios emerge for this industry depending on whether British or American weights are used, 3·78 on the former and 1·29 on the latter.

The quantity indices specified above can also be obtained by deflating the countries' gross output values for the various activities by appropriate international price indices, the British price weighted output index being obtained by deflating the American gross output values to an output value standardised in pounds sterling by means of an American quantity weighted price index:

$$\frac{\Sigma psqs}{\Sigma pkqk} \Big/ \frac{\Sigma psqs}{\Sigma pkqs} = \frac{\Sigma pkqs}{\Sigma pkqk}$$

and the American price weighted index being derived by deflating the output values by a British quantity weighted price index.[1]

$$\frac{\Sigma psqs}{\Sigma pkqk} \Big/ \frac{\Sigma psqk}{\Sigma pkqk} = \frac{\Sigma psqs}{\Sigma psqk}$$

This kind of formulation, by which United States – and by extension German – gross output values are deflated to a standardised £ sterling figure by means of price indices proved to have important operational advantages and has been adopted for the bulk of the comparisons. In principle, whenever possible, output values, labour force data and price ratios have been derived, for purposes of consistency and reliability, from a common source, often a production census. When, however, price ratios are not available from this basic source – as for instance in the case of construction – the above method has the advantage that alternative price indices can be introduced into the procedure without impairing the basic methodology.

In the case of a few activities, agricultural for instance, sources are available which specify quantities, values and average values of products which virtually exhaust the sector's output. Usually, however, sources from which the requisite information is culled are insufficiently detailed to provide quantities and prices for the bulk of items produced by the industry or sub-sector in question. Even where comparatively detailed information is available – as in manufacturing censuses – it is never possible to match between countries, for quantities and average values, a sufficient number of items to account for all the industry's output in both countries. In a few cases, a product may be produced in one country but not in another: there is no trace in the United Kingdom

[1] It can be seen that in this latter form the index would yield numerator and denominator output values standardised in dollars not pounds sterling. However, it is possible, in the following manner, to express both – as with the first formulation – in pounds sterling:

$$\frac{\Sigma psqs}{\Sigma psqk/\Sigma pkqk} \div \Sigma pkqk$$

This pounds sterling formulation has been adopted. It can be seen that the output ratio which it yields is identical to that given by the values expressed in dollars, i.e. to $\Sigma psqs/\Sigma psqk$.

of 'tobacco stemming and re-drying' a significant activity in the American tobacco industry.

As a result, the price indices used for deflating gross output to a common, standardised, basis are sometimes based on comparatively few products and/or a low coverage of an industry's output. Nevertheless, by using such price indices the assumption implicit in our methodology is that the price ratio between two countries for the non-covered items is identical with that obtained for the matched outputs.[1] The degree of reliability of the resulting productivity index depends on the number and output coverage of the selected (i.e. 'matched') products which feature in the price index.

Even where, as in the agricultural sector, volumes and values which are available for the three countries cover the bulk of output, the results are subject to important qualifications. In particular, the product groups which are available are in practice very broadly prescribed – for instance three kinds of meat are distinguished, beef and veal, pork, and lamb and mutton. The resulting comparisons for such 'products' thus relate not to prices but to average values. If, say, within such a group of items the United States produces a comparatively large proportion of high value, high quality products, the implication is that the resulting average value ratio will understate the purchasing power of dollars in terms of pounds sterling for the category in question.[2] Using these average values to deflate American gross output would understate standardised American output and productivity. This problem is a general one. It may be necessary, for instance, to compare *en bloc* quantities and prices of newsprint, though it comes in various types and qualities. Similarly, it proves necessary to measure numbers of airline passengers in aggregate, regardless of whether they are first or economy class.

Net output productivity comparisons

For reasons explained in chapter 2, international comparisons of sectoral productivity must be based on a *net* output concept. One way of measuring, and comparing between two countries on a standardised

[1] This qualification is not a special characteristic of the deflated output procedure described above. It applies with equal force to results obtained by weighting directly physical quantities with average values.

[2] This is one of the methodological grounds on which the 'industry approach' is thought to be less reliable than the 'expenditure approach' for yielding a measure of *per capita* national income: the comparison of 'average values' being contrasted with a more precise identification of specific goods, together with their prices, which is a feature of the 'expenditure' approach. However, by the same token, the output coverage achieved by the selected 'average value' products will tend to be greater than the coverage of each final expenditure category represented by the sample of individual items selected for price comparisons.

basis, the real *net* output of an industry, is to weight the various products produced in an industry first by estimated real value added *per product* of the domestic country and secondly by the real value added *per product* in the same industry in the other country. In practice, difficulties associated with estimating real value added for each of the principal products of an industry are likely to render this approach impracticable.[1]

Alternatively, an attempt can be made to deduct real raw material usage from real gross output for each industry in each country, so that two indicators, one for inputs and one for outputs, are needed. This is achieved by using 'double deflation', a technique in which real gross outputs of the industry are obtained on a standardised basis by the method described in the previous section, and from these are deducted real raw material usages obtained by a similar procedure, values of raw material usage being deflated, for the given industry in the two countries, to a common standardised basis by means of an appropriate international raw material price index.

In many activities output data are inadequate for yielding reliable estimates of real gross output per man. In the case of raw materials, statistical deficiencies in production censuses are even more acute, so that for most industries it is impossible to identify quantities and values for a sufficient number of raw material inputs to yield a reliable price index that can be used to deflate inputs in the two countries to a standardised basis. Moreover, in those cases where unreliable estimates of real raw material usage are deducted from not wholly reliable estimates of real gross output, statistical errors in the resulting real net output figures may be greatly accentuated. West writes that such net outputs are 'less trustworthy [than gross outputs] in a statistical sense' because 'net output per employee differentials . . . are highly sensitive to the relationship of input price differentials to output price differentials and, hence, are also highly sensitive to any errors in the price data'.[2] Nonetheless, the double deflation technique has been employed on occasion when making international output and productivity comparisons in manufacturing and in other sectors – for instance by Paige and Bombach, Mensink and West.

In view of the statistical problems associated with the use of the double deflation technique, especially the manner in which it may accentuate measurement errors, the method adopted in the present

[1] Mensink employed the technique when comparing British and Dutch productivity in selected industries. Even then, only Dutch weights could be derived and it appears this technique was chosen 'owing to the absence of data on international price ratios'. (*Statistical Studies No. 18, op. cit.*, p. 35.)

[2] West, *Canada-United States Price and Productivity Differences*, pp. 17 and 23. Paige and Bombach draw attention to this weakness of the double deflation technique (*A Comparison of National Output*, pp. 80 *et seq.*).

study consists of deflating to a standardised basis the net output values of an industry in the two countries, using the gross output price indices. Inherent in this method is the assumption that, for the activity in question, the relationship between the average cost of raw materials in two countries is identical with the gross output price index. There are in fact some theoretical reasons for the existence of a positive correlation between input and output price ratios: the former, together with the unit factor costs which characterise the relevant activity, being principal determinants of the latter.

It should be understood that this method does not assume identical technical, input–output, factor coefficients, for a given industry, in the two countries. Were this the case, net output productivity ratios would be identical with the gross output productivity ratios. In general net output productivity ratios obtained as described above differ from gross output productivity ratios for the same industry. To the extent that the basic assumption – an identity of output and input price ratios – is valid they reflect differences between countries in an industry's real net output. In turn, these differences are attributable, *inter alia*, to variations in the input–output coefficients which result from contrasting degrees of vertical integration, and industry output composition.

Tracing changes in comparative productivity ratios

It was explained in chapter 2 that it proved possible in the case of most sectors to make productivity comparisons for only a single base year. In the case of agriculture it was found best to focus attention on 1974. For manufacturing it proved necessary to go as far back as 1967–8 for the primary, base year, comparisons.[1] These years also provided the most opportune basis for international comparisons of the construction industry. In contrast, a recent year, 1977, was best suited to comparisons of the extractive industries, especially for oil and natural gas. For the public utilities, 1975 was used. In the case of transportation and telecommunication activities, US/UK comparisons were most conveniently made for 1972 and Germany/UK comparisons for 1970.

These various base year labour productivity measures were brought forward to 1977, or taken back to 1968, as the case dictated by official real output and labour force indices appropriate for the sectors in question. In the case of the output indicators, in order to move over time

[1] In principle it should have been possible to make comparisons between the 1974 British production census and the 1972 United States census of manufactures. In practice, British information pertaining to volumes and values of sales which, unlike the case in earlier censuses, was published not in the industry reports but in separate issues of the *Business Monitor*, proved inadequate for a large number of industries. Fortuitously, a full British census was available for 1968, and an American and German one for 1967, since when no major German census has been undertaken.

the results for the sub-sectors with which we have been concerned, it proved necessary in most cases to use component indices of the officially compiled index of industrial production. The consequential sectoral real output changes for the most part differed little from those yielded by series of sectoral contributions to GDP at constant prices. Where discrepancies occur the choice of output indicator has been based on an assessment of their relative reliability. In the case of labour force indicators primary use has been made of official series of numbers of employees.

For inter-country comparisons of certain sectors and sub-sectors, it proved possible to make direct estimates of labour productivity and comparative productivity for years other than the base year, results which afford some check on the methodology adopted for 'moving' productivity ratios over time.

Aggregation of sectoral results

To understand the aggregation methodology, it should be appreciated at the outset that an aggregate comparative productivity ratio is not simply a weighted average of the ratios of sub-sector and sectors. It is necessary first to calculate for each country the overall absolute productivity level – i.e. (standardised) net output per man – before comparing these levels between countries to yield an aggregate, overall, comparative productivity ratio.

Thus, overall[1] productivity is calculated for each country as:

$$P = \frac{O_1 + O_2 + \ldots + O_{\mathrm{n}}}{L_1 + L_2 + \ldots + L_n} = \frac{\Sigma_1^n O}{\Sigma_1^n L}$$

where O is (standardised) net output, L is the labour force, and 1, 2 . . . n denotes the component sectors (or sub-sectors). This expression may also be written as:

$$P = \frac{P_1 L_1}{\Sigma L} + \frac{P_2 L_2}{\Sigma L} + \ldots + \frac{P_{\mathrm{n}} L_{\mathrm{n}}}{\Sigma L}$$

where the series P represents absolute productivity levels (standardised net output per man) in the component sectors or sub-sectors. In short, aggregate labour productivity is a weighted average of component sub-sectoral or sectoral, productivity levels, the weights being the various activities' share of the labour force. The aggregate international productivity *ratio* is obtained at a second stage by relating the relevant aggregate productivity levels to each other.

[1] That is, overall productivity for a sector from sub-sector productivity levels, or for the industrial economy for component sectoral productivity levels.

It follows that aggregate international productivity ratios are determined not only by international sectoral and sub-sectoral ratios, but also by variations between the three countries in the structures of their economies. The nature of this 'structural' or 'composition' effect is such that an aggregate international productivity ratio may lie outside the range of the sub-sectoral, or sectoral, ratios. Even were output per man in each sector identical in two countries, aggregate productivity may differ if absolute productivity levels vary between sectors and the structures of the economies differ. The country having a comparatively large proportion of its labour force in high productivity (net output per man) activities would display the greater aggregate productivity. This aggregation procedure, which takes account not merely of component productivity ratios but also of absolute productivity levels, yields results which, apart from the qualifications given in chapter 2, should conform with those obtained by the 'expenditure method'.

Where the basic measurement method described in chapter 2 is used, all the data necessary for this aggregation procedure – sectoral and sub-sectoral labour forces, standardised net outputs and absolute productivity levels – are automatically available. However, it was impossible to apply the standard technique to all activities. For instance, the standard technique proved impracticable in such activities as oil and gas extraction, water supply, road haulage, ports, shipping activities, airlines and airports. In these sub-sectors, direct estimates of labour productivity ratios were made on the basis of *physical* units of output.

The problem which arises is how to integrate these ratios with those obtained for other sectors, since it is necessary, as shown, to aggregate on the basis of absolute sectoral productivity levels measured by (standardised) *values* of net output per man. The technique developed for dealing with this problem has been termed the 'reverse valuation' method for, unlike the standard procedure, we *start* in this case with the international productivity ratio, derived from physical units, and *finish* with a standardised net output figure which can be summed with those of other sub-sectors to yield the aggregate ratio.

Net output per man is available for all sub-sectoral activities in the United Kingdom. The reverse valuation technique consists, in the first instance, of multiplying this value, in the activity in question, by the international comparative productivity ratio (derived, say, from physical units) to yield for the same activity in the United States or Germany a value (thus standardised in pounds sterling) of the net output per man. In conjunction with the sub-sector's American or German employment level this in turn produces a surrogate net output figure (again standardised in pounds sterling) for the relevant sub-sector in the United States or Germany. Finally, these net output estimates can then be added to the other sub-sector net outputs to yield in turn an overall labour productivity level for comparison between countries.

The reverse valuation method is used to integrate productivity results derived from non-standard techniques into the general framework. Circumstances dictate, however, that it be employed in a wider role. As previously explained, it proved necessary to measure productivity levels and ratios for the various sectors in different years. When, as described, the standardised outputs (and labour forces) were 'moved' by means of appropriate indices to other years, the resulting net outputs, and net output per capita, remain valued in the prices of the relevant base year. In such a form, it is impossible to aggregate the sectoral outputs (and therefore productivity results) for a common year.

Again the problem is solved by the reverse valuation technique. The sectoral productivity ratios are aggregated for any given year using this procedure in conjunction with British sectoral net outputs[1] per head and sectoral civilian employment figures for the three countries.

[1] Sectoral contributions to GDP.

INDEX

agriculture, 56–8, 91ff
capital intensity in, 46–8
comparative productivity ratios in, 29ff, 38–40, 162; impact of double deflation on, 24
labour force quality in, 50, 106
market size of, 48–9
measurement of output in, 104–6
output and employment comparisons, 7, 15, 17, 31, 53ff
productivity of labour in, 4–6, 42, 43ff, 107; adjusted for hours of work, 23
strike action in, 51
structure of, 103–4
air transport, comparative productivity in, 151–3
see also transportation

Bombach, G., 3n, 11, 24n, 37n, 38, 39, 76, 105n, 130, 161
Britton, D. K., 58n

capital intensity, 45–8, 82ff, 96
see individual sectors
Caves, R. E., 12n
coal mining, 14, 15, 26, 36, 40, 59, 60, 92, 110ff
see also extractive industries
Cobb-Douglas formulation, 42
construction, 66–7, 91ff
capital intensity in, 46–8
comparative productivity ratios in, 29ff, 162; long-term changes in, 38–40
labour force quality in, 50
market size of, 48
measurement of productivity in, 127–8, 132–3
output and employment comparisons, 7, 34, 53
productivity of labour in, 4–6, 43ff, 128ff; adjusted for hours of work, 23
strike action in, 51
structure of, 127

double deflation,
impact of, 23–4
results in agriculture, 107–9
results in construction, 130–1
results in manufacturing, 124–5
double deflation technique, 13n, 16–17, 20, 23–4, 38, 161

electricity industry, measurement of productivity in, 137
see also public utilities
Elliott, D., 83n
employment comparisons by country and sector, 7
expenditure approach, the 10–11, 16, 164
extractive industries, 58–61, 91ff
capital intensity in, 46–8
comparative productivity ratios in, 29ff, 162; long-term changes in, 38–40
labour force quality in, 50
market size of, 48
output and employment comparisons, 7, 32, 53ff
productivity of labour in, 5–6, 43ff, 94; adjusted for hours of work, 23
strike action in, 51
structure of, 110–11

Frankel, M., 12n, 48
Frohn, J., 83n

gas industry, measurement of productivity in, 135–7
see also public utilities
Gilbert, M., 11, 12n

Heston, A., 12n
hours of work, differences in, 22–3, 24

industry,
scale of activity in, 96–7
size of, 82ff
vertical integration in, 83, 85, 97
industry approach, the 10–11, 16

Kendrick, J. W., 45, 57n
Kenessy, Z., 12n
Krause, L. B., 12n
Kravis, I. B., 11, 12n, 14n, 19, 46, 117n, 128, 129, 130, 133
Krengel, R., 83n
Kuhbier, P., 83n

labour,
problems of measurement, 14ff, 18–19
productivity comparisons of, 4–6, 11–14, 20ff
see also individual sectors

labour force quality, 49, 50, 97
labour inputs, measurement of, 17, 27, 49
Lee, K. S., 45
Lomask, J., 45

manufacturing, 61–6, 91ff
  analysis of productivity ratios in, ch. 6 *passim*, 121ff
  capital intensity in, 46–8
  comparative productivity ratios in, 29ff, 78–9, 115ff, 162; long-term changes in, 38–40
  labour force quality in, 50
  market size of, 48
  output and employment comparisons, 7, 33, 53ff
  output and productivity changes in, 65, 66
  productivity of labour in, 5, 12, 21, 41, 43ff, 63
  strike action in, 57
  structure of, 62
market size, 48–9
  see individual sectors
Mensink, G. J. A., 12, 161
motor vehicle industry, 15, 17, 92, 93

oil and gas extraction, 113
  see also extractive industries
Oppenländer, K.H., 83n
output,
  growth rates in, 52–5, 97–8
  measurement of, 15ff, 22–3
  see also individual sectors
output comparisons,
  by country and sector, 7
  method used to calculate, 158–62

Paige, D., 3n, 11, 24n, 37n, 38, 39, 76, 105n, 130, 161
plant size, 82ff, 97
posts and telecommunications, comparative productivity in, 153–6
  see also transportation
Prais, S. J., xiv, 12n, 82n
price weights, 20–2, 24, 158ff
public utilities, 67–9, 91ff
  capital intensity in, 46–8
  comparative productivity ratios in, 29ff, 162; long-term changes in, 38–40
  labour force quality, 50
  market size of, 48
  output and employment comparisons, 7, 35, 53ff
  productivity of labour in, 5–6, 43ff, 135ff; adjusted for hours of work, 23
  strike action in, 51
  structure of, 134–5

railways, 15, 39, 40, 71, 73, 95, 141
  comparative productivity in, 144–6
  see also transporation
reverse valuation technique, 19, 156, 164–5
road haulage, comparative productivity in, 147–8
  see also transportation
road passenger transport, comparative productivity in, 146–7
  see also transportation
Rostas, L., xiii, 3n, 11, 22n, 38, 39
Ruttan, V. W., 57n

sea transport, comparative productivity in, 148–51
  see also transportation
Second World War, effect on productivity, 93
services, 7–8, 19
Smith, A. D., 73n
strike incidence, 51–2, 97
  see also individual sectors
Summers, R., 12n

transportation, 69–74, 91ff
  capital intensity in, 46–8
  comparative productivity ratios in, 29ff, 162; long-term changes in, 38–40
  labour force quality, 50
  market size of, 48
  measurement of productivity in, 142–4
  output and employment comparisons, 7, 35, 53ff
  productivity of labour in, 4–5, 43ff, 70, 144ff; adjusted for hours of work, 23
  strike action in, 51
  structure of, 140–2

Uhlmann, L., 83n
United Nations International Comparison Project, 12

Vaccara, B. N., 57n
Verdoorn's Law, 52n

water industry, measurement of productivity in, 137–8
  see also public utilities
West, E. C., 12n, 161

Yamada, S., 57n
Yukizawa, K., 12n

RECENT PUBLICATIONS OF THE NATIONAL INSTITUTE OF ECONOMIC AND SOCIAL RESEARCH

published by
THE CAMBRIDGE UNIVERSITY PRESS

ECONOMIC AND SOCIAL STUDIES

XXVI *Urban Development in Britain: Standards, Costs and Resources, 1964–2004*
By P. A. STONE. Vol. I: *Population Trends and Housing*. 1970. pp. 436. £17·75 net.

XXVII *The Framework of Regional Economics in the United Kingdom*
By A. J. BROWN. 1972. pp. 372. £18·00 net.

XXVIII *The Structure, Size and Costs of Urban Settlements*
By P. A. STONE. 1973. pp. 304. £14·50 net.

XXIX *The Diffusion of New Industrial Processes: An International Study*
Edited by L. NABSETH and G. F. RAY. 1974. pp. 346. £16.25 net.

XXXI *British Economic Policy 1960–74*
Edited by F. T. BLACKABY. 1978. pp. 710. £29·00 net.

XXXII *Industrialisation and the Basis for Trade*
By R. A. BATCHELOR, R. L. MAJOR and A. D. MORGAN. 1980. pp. 380. £17·50 net.

XXXIII *Productivity and Industrial Structure*
By S. J. PRAIS. 1982. pp. 401. £20·00 NET

OCCASIONAL PAPERS

XXV *The Analysis and Forecasting of the British Economy.*
By M. J. C. SURREY. 1971. pp. 120. £6·50 net.

XXVI *Mergers and Concentration in British Industry*
By P. E. HART, M. A. UTTON and G. WALSHE. 1973. pp. 190. £8·75 net.

XXVII *Recent Trends in Monopoly in Great Britain*
By G. WALSHE. 1974. pp. 156. £8·25 net.

XXVIII *Cyclical Indicators for the Postwar British Economy*
By D. J. O'DEA. 1975. pp. 184. £9·75 net.

XXIX *Poverty and Progress in Britain, 1953–73*
By G. C. FIEGEHEN, P. S. LANSLEY and A. D. SMITH. 1977. pp. 192. £10·25 net.

XXX *The Innovation Process in the Energy Industries*
By G. F. RAY and L. UHLMANN. 1979. pp. 132. £7·50 net.

XXXI *Diversification and Competition*
By M. A. UTTON. 1979. pp. 124. £8·50 net.

XXXII *Concentration in British Industry, 1935–75*
By P. E. HART and R. CLARKE. 1980. pp. 178. £10·00 net.

XXXIII *State Pensions in Britain*
By J. CREEDY. 1982. pp. 102. £10·50 net.

NIESR STUDENTS' EDITION

1 *Growth and Trade* (abridged from *Industrial Growth and World Trade*)
By A. MAIZELS. 1970. pp. 312. £5·75 net.

2 *The Antitrust Laws of the U.S.A.* (3rd edition, unabridged)
By A. D. NEALE and D. G. GOYDER. 1980. pp. 544. £7·95 net.

4 *British Economic Policy 1960–74: Demand Management* (an abridged version of *British Economic Policy 1960–74*)
Edited by F. T. BLACKABY. 1979. pp. 472. £7·50 net.

5 *The Evolution of Giant Firms in Britain* (2nd impression with a new preface)
by S. J. PRAIS. 1981. pp. 344. £7·50 net.

REGIONAL PAPERS

1 *The Anatomy of Regional Activity Rates* by JOHN BOWERS, and *Regional Social Accounts for the United Kingdom* by V. H. WOODWARD. 1970. pp. 192. £6·75 net.

2 *Regional Unemployment Differences in Great Britain* by P. C. CHESHIRE, and *Inter-regional Migration Models and their Application to Great Britain* by R. WEEDEN. 1973. pp. 118. £6·75 net.

3 *Unemployment, Vacancies and the Rate of Change of Earnings: A Regional Analysis* by A. E. WEBB, and *Regional Rates of Employment Growth: An Analysis of Variance Treatment* by R. WEEDEN. 1974. pp. 114. £6·75 net.

THE NATIONAL INSTITUTE OF ECONOMIC AND SOCIAL RESEARCH

publishes regularly

THE NATIONAL INSTITUTE ECONOMIC REVIEW

A quarterly analysis of the general economic situation in the United Kingdom and the world overseas, with forecasts eighteen months ahead. The last issue each year contains an assessment of medium-term prospects. There are also in most issues special articles on subjects of interest to academic and business economists.

Annual subscriptions, £25·00 (home), and £35·00 (abroad), also single issues for the current year, £7·00 (home) and £10·00 (abroad), are available directly from NIESR, 2 Dean Trench Street, Smith Square, London, SWIP 3HE.

Subscriptions at the special reduced price of £10·00 p.a. are available to students in the United Kingdom and Irish Republic on application to the Secretary of the Institute.

Back numbers and reprints of issues which have gone out of stock are distributed by Wm. Dawson and Sons Ltd., Cannon House, Park Farm Road, Folkestone. Microfiche copies for the years 1959–80 are available from EP Microform Ltd, Bradford Road, East Ardsley, Wakefield, Yorks.

Published by
HEINEMANN EDUCATIONAL BOOKS

AN INCOMES POLICY FOR BRITAIN
Edited by FRANK BLACKABY. 1972. pp. 260. £5·95 net.

THE UNITED KINGDOM ECONOMY
by the NIESR. 4th edn, 1982.

DEMAND MANAGEMENT
Edited by MICHAEL POSNER. 1978. pp. 256. £5·50 (paperback) net.

DE-INDUSTRIALISATION
Edited by FRANK BLACKABY. 1979. pp. 282. £9·50 (hardback), £6·50 (paperback) net.

BRITAIN'S TRADE AND EXCHANGE-RATE POLICY
Edited by ROBIN MAJOR. 1979. pp. 240. £12·50 (hardback), £6·50 (paperback) net.

BRITAIN IN EUROPE
Edited by WILLIAM WALLACE. 1980. pp. 224. £10·50 (hardback), £4·95 (paperback) net.

THE FUTURE OF PAY BARGAINING
Edited by FRANK BLACKABY. 1980. pp. 246. £13·50 (hardback), £6·50 (paperback) net.

INDUSTRIAL POLICY AND INNOVATION
Edited by CHARLES CARTER. 1981. pp. 241. £14·50 (hardback), £6·50 (paperback) net.

THE CONSTITUTION OF NORTHERN IRELAND
Edited by DAVID WATT. 1981. pp. 227. £15·00 (hardback), £7·50 (paperback) net.